PENGUIN BUSINESS
# TIMELESS SKILLS

Nishant Saxena has had multiple stints as CEO, leading large businesses (Global CEO of the Erba-Transasia Group, India's largest in vitro diagnostics company; CEO—International at Cipla, India's leading pharmaceutical giant). Before that, he was the founder and CEO of an award-winning start-up.

Passionate about knowledge sharing, he curates 99reads.org, a collection of ninety-nine book summaries designed to make readers wiser. A prolific writer, he has contributed to top magazines and newspapers, delivered TEDx talks and is a member of Young Presidents' Organization (YPO), the global network of young CEOs.

An alumnus of IIM Lucknow and a distinguished alumnus of NIT Trichy, Nishant serves as a board member and chairman of the Nomination and Remuneration Committee at IIM Amritsar. A former certified trainer of *The 7 Habits of Highly Effective People* leadership course, he has lived and worked in six countries and travelled to eighty.

# ADVANCE PRAISE FOR THE BOOK

## CORPORATE

'Nishant's *Timeless Skills* offers more than just a list of traits; it serves as a practical guide grounded in real-world experience. In today's rapidly evolving and disruptive workplace, leadership is no longer a static concept. The skills Nishant discusses are crucial for leaders at all levels and across all industries to achieve their full potential. His hands-on insights reflect the challenges leaders face, offering actionable steps rather than abstract advice. By sharing his personal experiences, Nishant not only makes these skills accessible but also empowers leaders to navigate uncertainty with confidence, promoting leadership growth at any career stage'—**Rajat Dhawan, senior partner and India managing partner, McKinsey & Company**

'I've seen Nishant navigate challenges with wisdom, humility and an unwavering focus on growth—not just his own but that of everyone around him. His ability to turn everyday experiences into powerful lessons is what makes this book so special. Take the story of a talented manager whose career stalled because he avoided confrontation. We've all seen it play out—strengths like charm become weaknesses when not balanced with assertiveness. These stories hit home because they're real, relatable and packed with actionable insights. For anyone who wants to build a career and life that stands the test of time'—**Karan Singh, managing director, ACG Worldwide**

'I have seen first-hand how some careers take off while many get stuck and struggle for a break. So, it is a great idea to put together the timeless skills needed for career success.

With the author's rich experience in multinational corporations, Indian companies and start-ups, in India and abroad, he is uniquely positioned to write on this subject. His engaging style and real-life anecdotes bring the subject alive and make the book readable'—**Sanjeev Bikhchandani, founder and executive vice chairman, Info Edge**

'In *Timeless Skills*, Nishant Saxena delves into the critical yet often overlooked skills that can make or break a career. Drawing from his highly acclaimed workshop, this book synthesizes wisdom, customized for the Indian context, and presents it in an engaging and relatable manner. His chequered experience as a CEO of large global businesses shows through in the practical advice he curates for the reader. Whether you're an aspiring leader or a seasoned professional, this playbook will equip you with the tools to break through barriers, achieve your career goals and enrich your personal life'—**Shilpa Gentela, senior client partner, Korn Ferry**

'Easy, conversational and yet a brilliant book. Assimilates the knowledge of experts and brings in a new twist with a focus on the Indian diaspora. Nishant has broken down the elephant into bite-sized lessons—great for the new generation of leaders and a wonderful reminder and revision for leaders themselves'—**Preeti Razdan, CEO, Diageo Southeast Asia**

'Nishant has delved deep into a subject that will resonate with all managers and even proprietors who are at the middle of their careers. Being the editor-in-chief of one of the most-read newspapers, it was hugely challenging for me to balance my decision-making between being a CEO and a journalist. Reading through this book made me reflect on the dilemmas I had faced in the last decade. The anecdotes, suggestions and analysis presented in this book are a masterstroke'—**Sanjay Gupta, chairman and editor-in-chief,** *Dainik Jagran*

'I met Nishant when we were integrating his start-up with a part of Career Launcher, and he took on an executive role to run the combined business. He was always a great teacher, and his students remember his lectures on leadership and effectiveness till today. So, his idea of compiling all his learnings from a twenty-five-year-old career into a book is truly welcome. Would encourage all students who want to do well in the corporate world and in life to grab the book'—**R. Satya Narayanan, founder and chairman, Career Launcher**

'Nishant's reflections and stated examples from his career create a very interesting read for people seeking the nudges and motivation to stay on top of their careers'—**Umang Vohra, managing director and global CEO, Cipla**

'*Timeless Skills* strikes a deep chord and points out the frequently disregarded things that prevent people from advancing in their careers. With Nishant's extensive experience, he walks you through the seven key competencies that truly make a difference. I adulate this book because it's not just theory; it's full of real-life anecdotes and examples. I started thinking back on times in my own life when mastering one of these abilities may have had a significant influence. This book is a must-read and talks directly to anyone who is passionate about long-term success and job advancement and is direct and honest'—**Jayant Davar, founder and chairman, Sandhar Technologies**

'Nishant has done a wonderful job in picking lessons from various global experts and blending them with his own experiences and putting it all together as a practical book to help Indian entrepreneurs and managers significantly improve their performance. Amongst the many important points raised in the book, I particularly liked the emphasis on balance and self-awareness, two very important qualities that are not often talked about in books on leadership. The reader will enjoy this book and will great benefit from reading it'— **Sachit Jain, vice chairman and managing director, Vardhman Group**

'*Timeless Skills* is a gift from a very successful careerist to anyone who is going through a lean patch in their career. This superbly crafted book intuitively picks key themes, eloquently presenting them in easy-to-read and relatable chapters. Once you start, you cannot put it down. And go away with a possible pill for your career illness'— **Prabir Jha, founder and CEO, Prabir Jha People Advisory**

'India is on the road to becoming Viksit Bharat by 2047. A nation can only progress once it has a culture of innovation and skill, and India needs to have its code of skills. Nishant, in this book, has done brilliant work to write the way forward of the skill set required'—**B.L. Mittal, founder and chairman, Sasta Sundar**

'In *Timeless Skills*, Nishant artfully weaves his rich work experiences and extensive readings in management and social literature into a cohesive whole. Despite its extensive bibliography, the book maintains a refreshing practicality, emphasizing "balance" and prioritizing "execution and accountability" over mere strategy-making for managerial success. A must-read for anyone beginning their career journey and a valuable addition to the shelf of a seasoned executive or academic'—**Arun Khanna, former managing director, Johnsonville Asia-Pacific**

'*Timeless Skills* is a masterclass in leadership effectiveness. I have seen first-hand how technical expertise alone doesn't propel careers—it's the ability to adapt, balance priorities and overcome blind spots that truly differentiates leaders. This book breaks down those intangible yet critical skills that determine who rises and who plateaus. Packed with real-world insights, it offers a road map for professionals aiming to break through their career ceilings. I have seen how small behavioural shifts create exponential impact. This book is a powerful guide to unlocking your potential'—**Narendra Varde, managing director, IMCD Group**

'*Timeless Skills* is not only easy to read and understand but also accounts for the cultural context of Asian societies such as India's. Leadership skill is perhaps the most important attribute for growth in any sphere and this book will enhance this capability in a big way'—**Shashi Sinha, CEO India, IPG Mediabrands**

'I have known Nishant for the last twenty-five years. He always distinguished himself by his ability to deeply understand the key skills needed for success in a given role, synthesize the most relevant skills and share his insights with the larger team through corporate blogs or by becoming an in-house trainer. In this book, he has done that for the learnings of his entire corporate career. A must-read for anyone who wants to play the long game'—**Manish Maheshwari, Mason Fellow at Harvard Business School**

'*Timeless Skills* is a compelling and thought-provoking read that uncovers the hidden barriers preventing professionals from advancing in their careers. Through sharp insights, real-life case studies and actionable strategies, the book helps individuals identify blind spots, develop essential skills and accelerate their professional growth. Nishant has guided many professionals, including me, in their careers, and I have always aspired to learn more from him. This book is incredibly insightful—I only wish he had written it sooner so I could have benefited from it earlier'—**Harsh Pamnani, bestselling author of *From Unknown to Unforgettable*, *Booming Digital Stars* and *Booming Brands***

## ACADEMICIANS

'There are many leadership books, but they are mostly written by western authors with primarily western contextual knowledge. Nishant has rich CEO-level exposure in the Indian and emerging market context and has blended his own experiences with actual training-based insights and over 100 citations. Coming at just the right time as Prime Minister Modi envisions a Viksit Bharat or developed India. Highly recommended reading for any student or manager wanting to be a CEO one day'—**Prof. Bharat Bhasker, director, IIM Ahmedabad**

'*Timeless Skills* represents a seamless integration of concepts, short case studies and distilled experience to provide a useful guide to the critical skills that are needed to succeed in a corporate environment. I particularly liked the emphasis on balance and rejuvenation, two important skills that are often missed out in corporate discourse'—**Prof. Rishikesha T. Krishnan, director, IIM Bangalore**

'Having been in the IIM system for thirty years, I have seen some careers shine and many others hit the glass ceiling too soon. The gap is often in behavioural skills. Nishant, our star alumnus, erudite in both the corporate and academic world, has put together all his learnings to identify these gaps. Through real-life anecdotes, he also shows how to act on them. A must-read if you aspire to be a leader'—**Prof. Archana Shukla, director, IIM Lucknow**

'*Timeless Skills* by Nishant Saxena is a sharp, insightful guide for ambitious professionals navigating the complexities of career growth. With real-world examples and hard-hitting truths, Nishant unpacks the blind spots that high performers often overlook—habits that, if left unchecked, can stall their rise. This book isn't just about working harder—it's about working smarter, mastering collaboration and cultivating the emotional intelligence needed to lead. A must-read for anyone serious about long-term success in the corporate world'—**Prof. Debashis Chatterjee, director, IIM Kozhikode and author of *Leadership Chronicles***

'In an age of rapid change and fleeting trends, true leadership stands the test of time. *Timeless Skills* uncovers the enduring principles that have shaped great leaders across generations—wisdom that transcends industries and cultures. Replete with real examples, this book explores the foundational skills that make a leader truly influential: self-management, clarity, accountability and balance. Whether you're leading a corporate boardroom, a start-up or any collective, these skills remain your most valuable assets'—**Himanshu Rai, director, IIM Indore**

'Nishant has thrown open a treasure trove of super skills that professionals across levels need for sustained career advancement and fulfilment. The numerous caselets, examples and assessments crafted for readers make this book a richly packed resource, offering both a breadth of learning material and Nishant's deep wisdom regarding corporate careers. The book addresses the hard truths about what makes behavioural change difficult but necessary to maximize our individual potential and constantly grow our careers. It is a must-read for those who value investing in their personal and professional selves'—**Pramath Raj Sinha, founder and trustee, Ashoka University**

'I am honoured to introduce *Timeless Skills*, a powerful book that reveals why even the most promising careers can stall due to missing competencies or ingrained habits. It distils seven timeless skills through real-life caselets. Drawing on my own leadership experiences, I affirm that these principles—ranging from balance to rejuvenation—are critical for breaking through career ceilings and transforming common sense into effective, sustained success'—**Prof. Rajeev Kumra, director, T.A. Pai Management Institute, Manipal**

'Why do so many high-potential professionals hit a ceiling? They start strong—sharp, driven and technically brilliant. Yet, often, their ascent slows. What's missing isn't intelligence or effort—it's a set of often-overlooked behavioural skills that distinguish those who rise from those who remain stuck. Drawing from his highly rated *Timeless Skills* programme, Nishant Saxena blends hard-earned corporate wisdom with compelling storytelling and actionable insights. It's a mirror—showing the blind spots that sabotage careers and the skills that unlock new levels of influence, clarity and impact. *Timeless Skills* is your edge. Because, in the end, the ladder doesn't climb itself'—**Prof. Sunil Maheshwari, dean, IIM Ahmedabad**

'*Timeless Skills* explores seven essential skills that determine career success. Inspired by a highly rated training programme on skills for managerial effectiveness, the book talks about what blocks career success and what factors lead people to success. It translates common sense into practice through over fifty case studies drawn from the author's career experiences. Discover the real-life stories and practical insights that can transform your career. I recommend this book as a must-read for anyone looking to learn or teach about managerial effectiveness and career success'—**Dr Shailendra Singh, former director, IIM Ranchi**

'Nishant has applied the very quote he cites in the book to his own writing: "If you can't explain it simply, you don't understand it well enough" (Einstein). He has addressed the big problem in our careers by putting together the 7 *Timeless Skills* and explaining them in a simple and engaging way. I particularly liked the skill of focus, much needed in this era of distractions. I loved reading the book. I highly recommend it for reading about and application of timeless skills'—**Rajesh K. Pillania, India's 'Happiness Professor', Management Development Institute, Gurugram**

'Nishant delivers a stellar practical guide to management professionals on how to steer away from the most dreaded of all situations—a stalled career. I have had moments where I was unsure which career path would be meaningful and made choices under uncertainty. While reading *Timeless Skills*, I felt the rationale behind those choices unravel, making me sense that Nishant tapped into something profound. The book allows professionals to reflect and self-assess their situation. In a market cluttered with leadership books, *Timeless Skills* is a breath of fresh air that stands out as both personal and practical advice'—**Girish Mallapragada, chair, Kelley Undergraduate Honors Program, Kelley School of Business, Indiana University**

# TIMELESS SKILLS

## Playbook to Climb the Corporate Ladder

# NISHANT SAXENA

**PENGUIN**
**BUSINESS**

An imprint of Penguin Random House

PENGUIN BUSINESS

Penguin Business is an imprint of the Penguin Random House group of companies
whose addresses can be found at global.penguinrandomhouse.com

Published by Penguin Random House India Pvt. Ltd
4th Floor, Capital Tower 1, MG Road,
Gurugram 122 002, Haryana, India

First published in Penguin Business by Penguin Random House India 2025

ISBN 9780143466505

Typeset in Garamond by MAP Systems, Bengaluru, India
Printed at Replika Press Pvt. Ltd, India

www.penguin.co.in

*To my darling father, my constant cheerleader, my North Star*

# Contents

## Part 3: Conclusion and Exercises

# Preface

Why do careers stall? Strong performers at junior and mid-levels often fail to make the cut for more senior level roles. They display everything right in the initial years—passion, advocacy, intelligence and subject matter expertise. Indeed, in early years, each one shows the promise of a great career. But then, it's as if they suddenly hit a glass ceiling. While they continue to be valuable at their current levels, something remains amiss. There is a strong hesitation in promoting them, and they remain stuck at middle management. Why? Because the incremental skills required at more senior levels are deemed missing. And despite feedback, sometimes direct and sometimes subtle, the candidates do not improve. And so, alas, they remain trapped in the corporate hierarchy. Such a colossal waste of human potential.

So, what exactly are these missing skills that can make or break careers? We explored this question in our highly rated workshop, *Timeless Skills*, and this book draws heavily from that experience.

But first some background. To answer this million-dollar question, countless leadership and management books have been written. Some extremely impressive ones like *The 7 Habits of Highly Effective People* (by Stephen Covey)[1] or *Emotional Intelligence* (by Daniel Goleman)[2] or *The Leadership Pipeline* (by

Ram Charan)[3] based on solid research and author insights. And, of course, many dubious ones—regurgitating old wine, shallow and repetitive.

As a voracious reader, I often pondered how to make these models more complete. For instance, *The 7 Habits* offers valuable insights on empathy, but why doesn't it address self-regulation, which *Emotional Intelligence* covers so well? Or the more pragmatic pitfalls of high performers—like the tendency to keep winning even when the additional effort yields diminishing returns—a concept brilliantly explained in *What Got You Here Won't Get You There*.[4] In essence, how do we synthesize the wisdom of various masters?

Equally, it appeared to me, there were skills that have not been adequately talked about in leadership literature. Example, the ability to always strike a balance—one of the most underrated skills, but so critical to be successful. Being affirmative in chasing goals but also empathetic to understand others' viewpoints; being accountable for short term results while also ensuring long term health; working hard but also ensuring a rich life outside work and so on.

And then, of course, the Indian angle. Almost all the top twenty management books were written by American authors, drawing on research conducted in the USA. Indian empirical research in management themes is still woefully in its infancy. While many leadership skills may be universally applicable across cultures, there are distinct differences between Asian and Western approaches to leadership. The Hofstede Index[5] shows extreme differences between India and, say, United States (or United Kingdom, or more generally, the Western world). They are almost opposites in three out of six dimensions—Power Distance: Indians tend to rely more on their bosses for direction, favouring a top-down, directive style of communication.

Individualism: Indian culture leans toward collectivism, whereas the West celebrates individuality. Indulgence: In contrast to the West, Indian and broader Eastern cultures emphasize restraint, often marked by cynicism and even pessimism.

Hofstede is not alone. A recent *Harvard Business Review* (HBR) article[6] found marked differences between Indian and US leaders. When asked to prioritize their core responsibilities, shareholder return came first for US CEOs, but fourth for Indian CEOs (after 'building organizational culture' and 'being a guide to employees'). So, how can identical management frameworks suffice?

Beyond these gaps in content, the real challenge with management books often lies in their readability—how to deliver deep insights without being boring. When young students ask me for recommendations, I'm torn. The truly profound books can feel too heavy and have put many a young reader to sleep. But the simpler reads, while easy, often lack substance. What we need is the perfect balance: insights paired with storytelling, backed by research but easy to relate to.

That's what I admire most about my favourite authors—Yuval Harari, Bill Bryson, Richard Dawkins, Karen Armstrong, Michio Kaku and Will Durant. They have a knack for taking complex subjects and turning them into engaging stories. They have brought obscure topics to life for millions by simplifying the complex and crafting something wise and accessible; one that sticks with you long after the last page.

Through my blog and later in my executive role at a large corporation, I was often asked to deliver keynote lectures on leadership. I tried to present my own consolidated and customized framework, sprinkling what I thought was best from multiple sources, on my own experiences and anecdotal examples. I humbly shared stories of my own mistakes and learnings in the hope that vicariously, they would make the path of others easier. These were well received, whether in business schools or companies. And the discussion that followed enriched our understanding that further improved the content for future talks.

I started a programme in Cipla for our Top 100 leaders—*Timeless Skills*. Synthesizing the wisdom from multiple leadership literature, adding what I deemed was missing, adding my own examples and customizing for an Indian audience. The sessions were spread over the last Friday afternoon of every month for six months. This was extremely well received, scoring a Net Promoter Score (high scorers, less low scorers) of 94 per cent (NPS world class benchmarks are usually 80–85 per cent). More importantly, the managers of the participants confirmed a 16 per cent improvement in the behavioural skills being taught, a rare behavioural change through classroom intervention alone.

What caused this appeal? These skills were not new, and almost every participant had read of the importance of one or more of these in other contexts. And yet, they rated this course highly. For one, what is common sense is often not common practice. For example, while we all intellectually understand that clarity of thought is crucial for success, many of us still struggle to be crystal clear about what we want—whether in our work or in life in general. Complex problems confound us, and we get lost in the symptoms instead of finding the root cause. And so, we remain drifting through multiple non priorities, working hard but not reaching anywhere. *Timeless Skills* provides a structured understanding and multiple real-world examples of what worked and what didn't.

This was when Penguin suggested I turn these *Timeless Skills* into a book and offered to publish it. And here we are.

These are timeless skills, so in that sense, I can hardly claim to be the author. A curator maybe, a collector of wisdom from multiple sources. There is, however, a personal connection. Over two decades of management life, like all leaders, I have personally mentored multiple careers and seen some succeed and many remain stuck. I have given feedback to them on their missing skills and witnessed some blossom and grow, while most struggled to improve. It was as if something was holding them back, as if a part of them was not willing to improve. We will talk of these struggles—not just on the bad habits of otherwise good performers, but also on the challenges in improving. After all, how do you let go of the style that has made you successful thus far?

I have also evolved personally as a leader, starting as a starry-eyed analyst then and now with many years as CEO of large businesses. Across these twenty-five years, a lot of *feedback* has been given to me on my own missing skills, a lot of assessments, psychometric tests, behavioural interviews and 360-degree feedback. With each new piece of feedback begins the introspective, often painful yet enriching, journey of increasing self-awareness, developing missing skills, unlearning bad habits, and becoming a better manager and person.

Sometimes I was able to change and sometimes I thought I changed but others did not see the change. And sometimes, honest to heart, I could not change. We will also explore many of these direct, empirical learnings—stories from my own observations, struggles and experiences.

Welcome then to *Timeless Skills*. An agglomeration of proven success drivers. A framework for true effectiveness. A path to career and life enrichment. We have nothing to lose but our blind spots. The true seeker shall not be disappointed.

# The Journey Ahead: Chapter Synopsis

## Bringing It Alive

This book is about learning behavioural skills, and we all know that changing one's behaviour is anything but easy. Most training programmes, even those with excellent post training feedback score, fail to create a real lasting impact. So, in the actual workshop of *Timeless Skills*, we had a simple but effective learning guide: Learning by Teaching. At the end of every skill, participants were to teach it to a colleague or a loved one and get written feedback on both content and delivery. There were also exercises like self-assessments and start–stop to help participants make a clear personal action plan.

## 1. Why Exactly Do Careers Stall?

In most of my training sessions, I ask by a show of hands how many in the audience want to some day become a CXO. 80–90 per cent of all hands go up. And then I ask to look around and reflect, and then honestly answer, what percentage of the audience they think would make it to the highest echelons. The general response is 5–20 per cent.

What happened to the remaining majority—the hard working, knowledgeable and ambitious people? Why did they get stuck in 'middle management'? This chapter will explore this conundrum, offering real-life examples of otherwise capable individuals displaying bad habits or lacking key skills, ultimately hitting the proverbial glass ceiling.

## 2. So, What Can Be Done About It?

We will then show that these missing skills are generally coachable. While behaviour change is anything but easy, it is possible. It requires a Eureka moment, rigorous commitment, practise and constant feedback. Unfortunately, parts of our own brain shut off people who are willing to give transparent feedback.

If we can change, the benefits accrue both in our professional and personal lives.

## 3. Timeless Skills I: Self-Management

'If leadership is an art,' one of my coaches said, 'the artist's instrument is the self.' Indian sages talked of *atma-vichara* (self-contemplation) just as ancient Greeks, whether Epictetus or Plato, taught us to be self-aware. They also talked of self-control. Focus on things we can control; accept calmly things we can't control and be responsible for our actions.

Later, proponents of Emotional Quotient (EQ) like Daniel Goleman popularized three distinct areas: Self-awareness, self-regulation and self-motivation. We will discuss all these.

## 4. Timeless Skills II: Clarity

Clear thinking, the ability to see clearly through a problem and its root cause, is rare. Like a game of chess, we can see through what the main objective is, what will help us get there, what will stop us and how we can then make an action plan. Most CEOs are intelligent, capable and hardworking. This skill is the difference between successful people and merely busy ones. There are many biases and thinking errors that can cloud our judgement and our ability to see through the fog.

Clarity of thought is also reflected in clear, concise communication—a hallmark of great leaders.

## 5. Timeless Skills III: Focus

There was a time when the world talked about time management. But everyone has the same amount of time. What is more important is to carefully choose our big rocks, our most important priorities. A career is made or broken by four to five big projects, and not by the remaining drudgery. Choose these few wisely and ensure they get maximum attention.

This would mean proactively planning our week even before it starts, blocking time for the big rocks even before all the meetings and events clog the calendar. It means the ability to say no. It implies not being in the thick of thin things.

## 6. Timeless Skills IV: Accountability

If strategy is handled by senior management and execution by junior management, what is the role of the middle management? One core role is to take full accountability, not just of activities, but of the final outcome. If it is to be, it is up to me. If it is up to me, it will be. Good excuse plus bad result is still not equal to good result.

When someone asks me the role of a CEO, I jokingly answer: a glorified project manager. The hallowed job of strategy formulation takes hardly two weeks a year, the remaining is about execution. And execution must be managed, quarter on quarter, with multiple interdependencies, with multiple variables and so many uncertainties. Like a classic multivariate linear programme, this requires the science of planning.

Galvanizing a group of talented people will require gaining their trust, making them see a purpose bigger than themselves, tapping into their emotional zeal, clarifying the roles of each, resolving the many conflicts constructively and ensuring a robust system of feedback.

## 7. Timeless Skills V: Collaboration

Success in most roles requires collaboration with others. Yet, many brilliant individual performers fail to work with others. As we go up, breaking silos, getting cross functional teams aligned towards a common purpose and valuing the contribution of other functions become crucial for success. Collaboration starts with a mindset of abundance (there is enough in the world for all to win) and win-win thinking (I can only succeed if you also succeed).

This requires empathetic listening skills, allowing us to step into others' shoes before responding. Unfortunately, most of us listen with an intent to reply and not really with an intent to understand. The ladder of inference teaches us how to balance articulation (of our own views) with consideration (of others' views). Understanding *and* influencing.

## 8. Timeless Skills VI: Balance

Balance is perhaps the most underrated of all management skills. If leadership was about maximizing a single vector, artificial intelligence would take over some day. But almost in every sphere, it is about finding the elusive Goldilocks zone where multiple facets are balanced. For example, in the scale from empathy to aggression, too much on the left leads to seeking too much alignment, but too much on the right means losing followership. We must find that perfect balance—an art and a science.

This applies to every area—results orientation, balancing short-term gains with long-term business health; annual goal setting, weighing hard numerical targets against softer aspects like culture building; and team management, delegating without abdicating. The concept of balance is just as crucial in our personal lives.

## 9. Timeless Skills VII: Rejuvenation

How do we sustain high performance day in and day out over a 30–40-year career, where the real rewards come in the final 10–15 years?

Physical rejuvenation is a known science—exercising, reducing carbs and sugar intake, strengthening core and building muscles. Beyond that is mental fitness—recreating ourselves in the age of artificial intelligence and developing learning agility as we get into new roles. Similarly, financial planning to ensure we will have sufficient money to sustain our desired quality of life. And then, emotional fitness—having a few deep relationships we turn to when we're down, helping us rebound. Finally, we have now started to talk about spiritual coefficient, beyond IQ and EQ—a deep sense of self-awareness, alignment with deeper values and being at peace with our reality.

## 10. Afterthought

After discussing the 7 Timeless Skills, we conclude with whether these are indeed sufficient and how to live in an imperfect world.

As a playbook, we also provide space for the reader to do a guided introspection and personal action planning.

# Bringing It Alive

The little secret of the training industry is that most programmes don't work in achieving actual behavioural change.[1] The post training feedback, which measures reaction to the workshop or how participants feel immediately after the workshop, generally gets a good score. But whether most people actually show behavioural change over a period of time is an all together different story. People may develop an awareness about new ideas, even appreciate what was taught. But internalizing it, changing behaviour or developing a new life skill is very difficult and various models have tried to estimate the true impact of training.[2]

In the Timeless Skills workshop, we were able to deliver a significant change, evidenced not just by the 94 per cent Net promoter score, but by a 16 per cent improvement in specific behaviour of the participants as rated by their managers.

Two things worked well.

## Learning by Teaching

'If you can't explain it simply, you don't understand it well enough'—Albert Einstein

This is a very old technique[3] where participants, after learning core concepts, try to teach these to someone else who is important to them. In the process, as the new student asks questions, the participants clarify their own understanding. The learning also gets reinforced by this repetition. Most importantly, when we teach someone important who we will keep meeting again and again, we end up taking a public stand, a commitment, and this acts as a powerful incentive to implement what we have learnt.

I picked this up from *The 7 Habits of Highly Effective People*. I loved the training so much that I applied for and got selected to be a trainer myself, along with my corporate job. As part of becoming a trainer, I was supposed to informally train someone important. And so, on many evenings, I would discuss the main concepts separately with my mother, my wife and a dear colleague. The discussion would delve into how difficult it will be in practise to focus only on our circle of influence and ignore what is outside our control. Or how tempting it is to listen to respond, instead of listening to truly understand. These discussions outside the classroom reinforced the ideas in my own head. Plus, having presented myself as a trainer of these skills, I would consider myself a hypocrite if I did not practise them myself. Hence the self-pressure to practise what we preach. Over the years, my annual assessments have consistently highlighted these as my strengths—I'm generally cool and calm, rarely fazed by uncontrollable external factors. And that I am an empathetic listener. So, the reinforcement method works.

We implemented Learning by Teaching in the Timeless Skills workshop and participants gave rave reviews. Some taught these concepts to a co-worker, others to their team, a few to their kids and one brave lady even to her husband. To ensure robustness, we asked participants to get a note from their 'student' detailing what was taught and how it was delivered. Some of these are affixed here (see page 203) with their permission.

So, my suggestion as you go through the book is this:

- After every few pages, as you ruminate through an interesting concept, please first make a handwritten note at the back of the book. There are empty pages attached called, Notes for Self.
- Then teach it to someone important to you—at work or in life. Ask them to write what you taught and how it was taught. There is space provided at the end of the book.
- Repeat for all important concepts. Pick up only those that really appeal to you. Don't be in a hurry to finish the book. The actual workshop was spread over six months to give time to participants to practise what they were learning.

## Personal Action Planning

After every chapter, look at the summary. Then fill up the personal action plan at the end of the book:

- Start: What new behaviour will you start exhibiting. Look at the concepts which most appeal to you. Recall also the feedback you have received so far in work and from loved ones. What have they called out as your development areas?
- Stop: Identify which current behaviour is unhelpful and commit to stopping it.

Each chapter will also include a self-assessment. Try going through it when you are relaxed. These will help answer the 'so what' question: We have learnt this, so what is the impact in our lives. Please try filling it up—introspect and answer the questions in the space provided.

# Part 1 | Introduction

## Why Exactly Do Careers Stall?

BB was an intelligent and collaborative manager, well-versed in the industry and financial markets. Diligent and detail-oriented, he ensured his work was always thorough. His outcome-driven mindset, strong team management skills, and ability to charm customers with win-win solutions made him a valuable asset. He also had a soft yet persuasive leadership style that resonated well with his bosses, and he consistently maintained a strong grip on his numbers.

However, his desire to stay in everyone's good books often held him back. He struggled to strike the right balance between being approachable and assertive—hesitating to take bold stands if they risked being unpopular. Confrontations with erring customers or cross-functional peers were avoided rather than tackled head-on. And projects that were ambigious or involved challenges got delayed. While his many capabilities still made him valuable at his current level, the perception of not being assertive enough prevented him from advancing into senior leadership. Over time, he watched younger colleagues climb the ladder while he remained in place, despite his many talents.

In the *Timeless Skills* program, he committed to work on two aspects:

Freedom to Choose: Freeing himself from dependencies (including what others say about him) that led to frustration or stagnation.

Overcoming Procrastination: Tackling ambiguous and unattractive projects with confidence and building a personal system of execution.

The transformation was remarkable. Today, in meetings, BB is vocal on his opinions and challenges others. He takes targets and gets things done. This propelled him up the corporate ladder and he was given a much wider geography to run.

All of us have seen careers stalling. The popular heroes in college days do not turn out to be heroes in their work lives. Young, smart analysts in the corporate world show potential in their first few years but fail to make the cut for serious CXO level and remain stuck in the middle layers of the corporate hierarchy. Why?

I think it is because of two primary reasons:

- Not giving up on old bad habits
- Not learning new skills

Let us discuss these one by one.

## The Bad Habits of Good Performers

People become successful because *of* certain good habits: technical competence, intellect, knowledge and hard work to name a few. But alongside these strengths, the same people often carry some toxic bad habits, which, despite their success so far, go unchecked. They are not perfect, but their strengths overshadow their weaknesses. Think Steve Jobs: brilliant creativity but questionable people skills (would tear and throw presentations on the face of his employees).

These blind spots, if left uncorrected, can put serious brakes in career. Unfortunately, while it sounds simple and logical, successful people are often in denial. Their confidence in their own talent and their ability to deliver results ironically makes them much more difficult to change. In fact, they often credit their weakness as being responsible for their success.

Marshall Goldsmith, in his seminal book *What Got You Here Won't Get You There*, gives the example of Harry[1] who was successful because of his smartness, his ability to always deliver his numbers and his sincere care for the company. However, he was also a poor listener, even after accounting for the fact that his colleagues—intimidated by his quick mind and creativity—did not really expect him to listen to them all the time. And like the same person we usually are in and out of office, his wife and kids also confirmed he usually did not hear a word of what they said. But for Harry, this was almost his key to success. He was convinced that by shielding himself from the 'stupid' ideas of his co-workers, he was actually preventing his fertile brain from getting polluted. His other defence was the risk of over-correction. If he started to listen too much and to speak less, his creative ideas could ultimately dry up. As his coach, Marshall had to explain the difference between correlation and causality—Harry was successful due to his sheer talent and happened to be a poor listener, but one wasn't the cause of the other. In fact, Harry would probably not go any higher in the corporate world if he did not correct his listening.

Poor listening can also take the form of starting with a no/but/ however. In a more elegant version, people will say 'I agree with you, but . . .' before proceeding to contradict the other person's ideas. In essence, they are saying, 'I am right, you are wrong.' In essence, they have not really listened empathetically to understand.

Marshall continues to offer twenty-one such blind spots. Some people have the bad habit of *Winning Too Much,* which becomes toxic when we start wasting time and energy to win in every trivial issue. We may end up winning that specific battle only to realize it was not worth it. Think about how often we try to win every single argument with our spouse, wasting time and energy and spoiling a very important relationship.

Some bosses have the bad habit of *Adding Too Much Value* wherein they will keep giving their inputs to show that it is their initiative. This probably improves an idea by 10 per cent but reduces staff commitment by half because the sense of ownership in others is gone.

Then there is the toxic habit of *Making Destructive Comments.* We all know of wisecracks who think they are being smart or witty, but the receiver of those comments is devastated. A manager should be demanding but not demeaning.

In my own experience, I have seen many young and passionate people have difficulty in collaboration, especially with their cross-functional peers. In the beginning of their career, it works fine because they bring the issues to their managers who bust those barriers. In fact, they can move with speed by avoiding the time-consuming work of getting a broad-based consensus. But as these same employees get promoted, they struggle with aligning cross functions because all this while they had seen the functions as adversaries who were slowing them down. As a result, when management convenes annual promotion meetings, the comments made about them are: 'smart go-getter but lacks maturity for the next level.' This stalls their career progression.

## Learning New Skills

When I became a CEO, my mentor, a seasoned South African, quipped, 'Now is the time to move from being the smartest to being the wisest.' You see, I was this young Chief Finance Officer (CFO) under him, very proud of my analytical skills. And in meetings, I would slice and dice data and quickly rubbish business proposals. Even if business results were good, I would hastily find that one piece which was not doing well and highlight it, much to the chagrin of our sales director. I tried to be the first to answer questions and use my articulation skills to make compelling cases.

But as the CEO overseeing operations in eighty countries, I quickly realized that I couldn't possibly know what was right for, say, Colombia or New Zealand—certainly not as well as the local country manager. And I would not have the bandwidth to learn very deeply about every single country. The complexity of business often meant the risk of working hard but going nowhere, coming home exhausted each evening only to frustratingly realize that little had been accomplished. And constantly being under pressure that I did not know enough.

Therefore, the quest for being wise entailed choosing the few priorities to focus on which, if done well, would deliver step-change results. It meant getting the right talent—much smarter, with better contextual knowledge and hopefully complementary to my skills—who could actually solve individual problems in individual countries. It meant choosing battles where it was okay to lose because the incremental reward of winning was not commensurate with the incremental effort to win. Overall, the humbling realization sank in: There was so much I didn't know that it was best to keep listening and learning and developing next level talent.

The point of this little anecdote is that these aspects— hiring smarter people or listening or letting go—were new skills hitherto not as crucial in my career. But these would become make or break in my new elevated role. The Western style of management has traditionally celebrated the aggressive go-getter that accentuates self-expression and, only now, is waking up to 'quiet leadership.'[2] We will talk more about listening later. But for now, learning this incremental skill also meant unlearning my innate temptation to be the first to answer.

In his path-breaking book, *The Leadership Pipeline*, the famous Indian origin management guru Ram Charan identifies career transitions where new skills and perspectives are required.[3] Consider the typical career progression: An analyst becomes a manager, then a manager of managers, followed by a function head, and so on. Each of these levels requires a very distinct set of incremental skills. People need to start exhibiting these new skills *before* they can be considered for promotion. You could be delivering good performance at the current level but may still not be considered for the next level because the skill set requirement for these two levels is different.

Let's start from when individuals join an organization at an entry level, fresh out of university, say as an analyst. What will make them successful? Generally, the answer is hard work and subject matter knowledge. As long as the quality of output is good and on time, the entry level employee is considered decent.

In a few years, these young analysts are considered for promotion. Maybe become a manager of people, responsible not only for their own output but also for the collective output of their team. Now suddenly, new sets of skills start mattering. These would include planning (breaking down overall deliverable into smaller chunks with a time bound action plan), delegating (to their own team members based on interest and capability and then monitoring closely), recruiting (hiring right talent fit for the role), motivating, monitoring, coaching and, most importantly, taking full accountability of final results, without any excuses.

The aha! moment is realizing that most of these skills aren't core requirements at the previous level of individual performance. One can still be a great analyst without exhibiting any of these incremental qualities. But they become a *sine qua non* (essential) as we move up. So indeed, what got us here, won't get us there. Successful managers learn new skills as they move up, change their perspective on what is important and reprioritize where to spend time.

## Why Do We Not Learn and Unlearn Readily?

Sadly, many people do not make that transition. We get promoted because of our past successes, so the default mindset is to continue with the behaviour that delivered success. We have all seen examples of great salesmen who are unable to scale up to become great sales managers. They still want to close the deal themselves, they want to meet every customer themselves, no new sales rookie under them measures up to their standards. So instead of coaching the new salesperson, they end up spending a lot of time doing the subordinate's job. Delegation is anathema to them because they have always prided themselves on being a doer. For a while, this model may still work, but they soon run out of bandwidth, unable to handle wider geographies or larger teams. While they were great individual salesmen, they become, at best, an average sales manager. And hence, they can't get promoted further to more senior levels.

Sometimes, they are also insecure and do not inherently desire to develop their subordinates. They are worried that their own role could get obviated if the next level person is seen capable. They may still help the subordinates do well in the current role but not actively develop them for the next level. And so, many careers die a premature death, doing well but not going any higher.

Unfortunately, in most companies, leadership development is not given as much attention as strategy development or operation management. In many companies, managers are rewarded mainly on results and much lesser on the 'how' of results. As long as the money keeps coming in, leadership does not care much whether the next layer of leaders is being groomed or not. Sadly, we do not see people honing behavioural skills.

Even our education system hardly coaches us on softer managerial and leadership skills. As a result, people remain 'technically strong' and hardworking but just don't make the cut for higher echelons of management. Think about all the classes we had in school—maths, science, history, English. But classes on listening? On collaboration? On rejuvenation? Hardly any.

My first campus job was in the iconic Procter & Gamble (P&G). Somebody had remarked that P&G had given more CEOs to Fortune 500 firms than even Harvard Business School. One reason for its strong leadership pipeline was their motto when I was an employee there: *Pay for Performance but Promote for Potential.* Meaning, if employees do well in their current roles, pay them well and give them a good bonus. But good performance at current level is only a necessary condition, not a sufficient condition to consider employees for promotion. To be considered for the next level, employees need to start exhibiting potential or new skills required for that higher level *before* they actually get promoted.

In P&G, one of the jokes was that many people who were the fastest to be promoted to the first one or two levels almost never made it to serious leadership levels like CXO. Because the skills that gave them initial success were not sufficient for the next few levels. Sadly, seeing how much early success they got because of their existing skills, they were neither willing to let go nor willing to experiment with new thinking. And so, they stagnated at middle level.

# Summary

- Careers stall because of dual failure—failure to unlearn bad habits that have been carried so far and failure to learn new skills needed for higher levels.
- *Because of* and *In spite of* behaviour—people succeed because of some strengths and in spite of some weaknesses.
- Typical blind spots include poor listening (listening to reply instead of to understand), excessive competitiveness (trying to win even when incremental effort is more than incremental reward), adding too much value (to the point of taking away others' ownership), making destructive comments (which we find witty, but others find offensive), poor collaboration (especially at peer level), etc.
- At every level of hierarchy, incremental skills are needed. Entry-level success is based on hard work and subject knowledge, but management roles require 'softer' skills like planning, delegating and coaching.

## Food for Thought: Self-Assessment

1. Reflect on a colleague who, despite reasonable performance, was stalled for promotion due to a perceived lack of potential. What specific qualities or skills were missing? How did this experience shape my perspective on the factors that drive career progression?

2. Based on personal experience, what are the core competencies or abilities that have consistently contributed to my achievements and recognition?

3. In moments where it becomes evident that my prior skills are inadequate for the next level, what is my reaction? What steps do I take to build the necessary competencies for advancement?

4. Identifying weaknesses and blind spots through 360-degree feedback: When analysing feedback from managers, peers, subordinates and self-assessments, as well as benchmarking against peers, what are my areas of self-improvement? Do I embrace these, or is there defensiveness around them?

5.  Reflect on situations where hesitation to support a subordinate's growth stemmed from fear or insecurity. How did this impact team dynamics and overall performance? What strategies can be adopted to change this?

6.  How have colleagues who embraced negative feedback and actively worked on their weaknesses influenced perceptions of self-improvement? What changes can I make to adopt a similar mindset?

# 2

# So, What Can Be Done About It?

There is some great news and some not-so-great news. Here's the latter: Most of the skills needed to climb the corporate ladder are not just cognitive. In other words, they are not like computer programming, financial analysis, foreign languages or technical know-how that you can learn in a classroom just to tick a box.

What are the real skills for moving up? They are generally behavioural—and that makes them a bit trickier to pin down. They require a change in our basic attitude and thinking process, and this is rarely easy and rarely a linear journey.

But there is good news too. Learning these skills is not insurmountable. Behaviour change may not be easy but can certainly be achieved if we persevere.

## How Do We Change Attitude and Behaviour?

I curate a website on books, 99reads.org. The idea is to get our younger generation to read, so I have personally selected some iconic books across multiple genres that are engaging to read and can help readers become wiser. For each book, I pen down a short summary and review. I was talking about this website during a guest lecture at a business school when a young girl stood up, complimented the effort, and promised to start the habit of reading good books. Indeed, later she wrote to me that a lot of her time was wasted aimlessly on social media, so she was making it her new year resolution to read good books and had even ordered a couple of books online. But alas, during the year, her existing entrenched habits seemed to have taken over again. She confided that, along with her friends, she was back to scrolling lazily through WhatsApp and Instagram while those unopened books waited for them.

Many of us have tried to enlist a change in attitude or behaviour (either ours or someone else's) in our new year lists or annual performance assessment goals: 'I will be more in control of my emotions' or 'We will make employees more accountable' or 'I will be a better listener,' etc. However, we are also regularly frustrated that our attempts to change behaviour so often end up in failure—with old habits dying really hard. It may be because we are trying to solve the wrong problem.

Attitude (pre-disposition to behave in a particular way, which then leads to behaviour) is just a symptom, governed by what we have seen, known ('cognition') and felt ('affect') over a period. Our past experiences result in mental paradigms that affect how we behave. Deep-rooted values, beliefs and biases are at the core of a demonstrated behaviour. For example, an employee with bitter memories of being innovative (e.g. being ridiculed) may then show conformist behaviour. Similarly, a person with an inherent low self-esteem ('mindset') will obviously find it difficult to 'behave' with confidence. Or, in the above anecdote, many students find most academic books boring and too theoretical with little practical value add. It's no wonder, then, that they've developed an aversion to reading.

Ergo, to change attitude or behaviour, we first need to change mindset.

Back in my consulting days, a Fortune 100 European food giant wanted us to coach their sales team to focus on profit, and not just volume sold. I asked a simple question: 'Do you reward them for profits?' Their nonchalant reply went, 'Sales teams worldwide are rewarded on volume!'

Well, if pushing volume, even unprofitably, is what gets them rewards, of course they would focus on volume. A classroom pep talk will not change anything if the incentives stay the same.

Another large multi-national company (MNC) asked us to help develop their middle management layer so that they could become proactive problem solvers, instead of their current (perceived) habit of escalating all issues to their managers. When we dug deeper, we realized that, in the past, solutions suggested by middle managers generally received lukewarm support from the top, and when things went wrong, these managers were severely reprimanded. Hence the 'pre-disposition' (read about 'learned helplessness'[1]) to delegate any thinking and problem-solving upwards.

So, how do we change such a deep-rooted mindset? There is little evidence that classroom training can be a panacea. It may result in some degree of awareness but not really a sustained change in behaviour. It would be wishful thinking to suggest that someone who is perpetually short-fused can go to a two-hour anger management workshop and become calm and composed for the rest of his life. Pep-talks, at best, create a transient high.

What we seek is first a change in our mindset, our paradigm, our view of the world. This kind of paradigm shift comes first from real experience (e.g. some very high personal price paid for getting angry) and only then insights (e.g. the knowledge that biologically, when we are angry, we harm ourselves much more than others) and tools (alternate and positive ways to release pent up frustrations and emotions, instead of losing temper). Just teaching yoga or meditation ('tools') will not help if the person's mind-set has not changed vis-à-vis anger.

Let me tell you the real story of the CEO of a publishing giant in India. He was known for his 'short temper' and I was called in as a leadership coach. Before we could help him control his public outbursts, we needed to understand the fundamental mindset causing his caustic behaviour. In interviewing him and others, we found the following paradigms that he subconsciously believed in:

- 'Many of my people (especially those I tend to lose patience with) are incompetent or insincere.'
- 'My public lashing drives the message that shoddy work will not be tolerated.'
- 'I like the Steve Jobbish image of a slightly moody, powerful, passionate person!'

Before the actual behaviour could change, this mindset needed to change, and that too at the subconscious level. We took each of his three beliefs and tried to challenge them.

Perhaps the perceived incompetence in his staff had more to do with broken processes, unclear expectations, lack of training and guidance or the sheer complexity of the task. In any case, having been in the role for many years, he also needed to take a share of the blame if many of his staff were incompetent. Similarly, a public message on quality of work could still be effectively delivered without a public lashing (by giving feedback on instances without mentioning the individual). We can be demanding without being demeaning. Finally, we discussed the difference between 'because of' and 'inspite of' behaviour (Was Steve Jobs successful 'because of' his anger or 'inspite of' it?).

We need to change our mindset, paradigm and belief system; otherwise, our behaviour will feel justified, leading us to relapse into it. How do we change if our 'rational' mind is subconsciously justifying our actions? For example, a wife who is convinced that her mother-in-law has ill feelings towards her may tend to show disrespectful behaviour—in her mind this is a justified tit for tat. Till this thought (real or imagined) remains in her mind, sustained behaviour change will be impossible. I would wager that just a pep talk to her—say on the importance of giving respect to elders—won't bring much change. Note also that her mindset will be shaped by her *perception,* more than by any objective reality. Therefore, what the mother-in-law says in her defence is inconsequential versus what the wife 'sees' her doing. It's a classic case of 'walking the talk.'

Brain-based learning, the crossroad of management and neuroscience, has identified our limbic brain as the seat of emotions, and hence the origin of a lot of our 'reflex' behaviour. This behaviour can be changed but the process requires moving away from directly attempting behaviour change to focussing first on mindset change. Typically, it is a four-step process:

- **Awareness:** Of what needs to change and what mindset is causing this behaviour
- **Deep Self-Motivation:** Inner desire to truly change habits, to improve
- **Long-term Practise:** At least for six to nine months (consciously trying to cultivate a new habit)
- **Constant Feedback:** By a mentor/ buddy (who gently corrects when the individual is reverting to old

ways and claps when the individual is exhibiting the
'right' behaviour, and with whom there is no ego wall)

Generating this deep self-motivation and convincing individuals
that change is indeed in their own interest is often the most
difficult. For that we need to create instances and stories which
bring a paradigm shift, a change in the mindset itself. It's not
typical surface level stuff; we're talking about motivations so
sneaky they're hiding in our subconscious. This isn't just about
changing because someone said so; it's about unearthing the
mindsets and biases buried deep within our subconscious brain
and altering them.

Freud used to call it Id.[2] He gave the example of a child
who wakes up its mother in the middle of the night to relieve
itself. Technically, this is selfish and insensitive behaviour that
does not care about the comfort of the mother. But the child,
not yet knowing about selfishness or selflessness, just wants
instant gratification. That is Id, our unadulterated state.

To affect a change in behaviour, we need to engage with
this true self.

Sometimes a trigger event helps change paradigm. My
father was a chain smoker who struggled with giving up the bad
habit. But one day my little daughter complained of wheezing
because of the smoke in the house. She asked him if he would
be willing to give up smoking for her sake, and with tears in his
eyes he committed to it and hardly smoked ever since.

For others, the trigger event may be a jolt in the form of a
health scare or death in the family. One of my team members, DK,
ever the foodie, got a 'wake-up call' pathology report showing
excess sugar and cholesterol for both him and his wife. The
doctor warned of severe consequences and terrible associated
risks if these were not corrected. Shaken, both husband and

wife adopted healthy eating and living, and managed to lose 10 kilograms each in six months under professional guidance.

In organizations, an intelligently designed 360-degree feedback can act as the same wake-up call.

Even so, it is not easy. To move an inch outside, we must move a mile inside. First our own change has to be sustained, only then will people start noticing the change.

In reality, I have seen both success and failure stories. After getting direct feedback and a nurturing environment to grow, many of my managers have improved in areas like taking accountability, collaboration and focus. Clarity of thought is a tad more difficult to develop since it is closely related to sharpness of thinking itself.

I have also seen people get hardened and not wanting to change. They intellectually understand the incremental skills that are needed to improve and even try to adopt them. But they keep falling back to their old behaviour. In one of my stints, our HR leader would mention to all that in her younger days she had very rough edges which she had improved over the years. But people around her would smile knowing that, despite all her other strengths, her rough edges and poor listening continued, making collaboration difficult and attrition high in her own department. So, even the head of human resources, with all her other qualities, failed to drive a sustained change in her own behaviour.

In most cases of failure, the fundamental paradigm did not change. And so, behaviour change was not sustained. Unfortunately, corporate folklore suggests this hardening is often correlated with age and experience, with senior leaders finding it even more difficult to change deeply rooted behaviour. I heard somewhere that an intelligent definition of aging is when we become less adaptable. Think of how flexible we were—

mentally and physically—in our younger days. Willing to accept contrarian views, willing to compromise, lesser ego. Often, with age and experience, we start holding on to our beliefs and biases. So much so that, as we grey, we often use our knowledge and life experiences to selectively reinforce our existing biases and to downplay other views, thereby getting even more hardened.

Does it always have to be this way? Certainly not. There are enough examples of people in their sixties who retain a childlike adaptability, curiosity, open mindedness and humility. Just as there are teenagers who already start exhibiting a closed mindset and obstinacy. We just need to be mindful that with age and experience, we need to guard against possible hardening of mindset.

The other watchout is that, in times of stress, our ingrained bad tendencies come out of the closet. Almost all psychometric assessments try to evaluate us on our inherent beliefs which can still be controlled and camouflaged till everything is going smooth but emerge when we are off guard or vulnerable. For example, a very popular self-assessment in corporate world, Hogan's HDS inventory[3] identifies our potential derailers that start showing when there is pressure.

Read the brilliant book *Incognito* by Stanford neuroscientist David Eagleman, which explores the secrets of the unconscious mind.[4] The conscious and the unconscious mind; the rational and the impulsive mind; the part of mind that delays gratification and exercises self-control for the greater good versus the part of mind which wants instant pleasure—these are independent and often in conflict. It's almost like many competing sub agents within our brain trying to deliberate on a course of action and then usually, when we are in our full senses, our conscious mind decides which path to go with. But there are instances where consciousness fails to decide. For example, in experiments with rats, when placed in front of food that also delivers an electric shock, the poor rodent gets stuck at a certain distance from the food, unable to move any closer or farther away. The conscious brain is moving him away due to shock while the unconscious is moving him to the food due to desire, and at that distance, the pull just matches the push.

Think of a corporate meeting room where you have *Team Long-Term Vision* on one side of the table and *Team Instant Profit* on the other. Team Long-Term Vision advocates for strategic planning, and investments in sustainability. On the other hand, Team Instant Profit wants to launch new products quickly and increase quarterly returns.

Now, imagine these two teams debating a risky new project with high potential but equally high costs. Team Vision pulls back, cautioning patience and incremental progress. Team Instant Profit, in contrast, lures forward, urging a big launch now for immediate gains. Ultimately, the CEO—the 'conscious mind'—sits at the head of the table, trying to choose a direction. But if the arguments are perfectly balanced, the CEO is stuck in decision limbo—like that poor rat between food and shock. And so, the company stands still, pulled by ambition, pushed back by caution and perfectly positioned for . . . absolutely nothing.

I have personally experienced this. My coach gathered 360-degree feedback from my team and gave me excellent advice on how to correct my unhelpful behavioural tendencies. I readily accepted the feedback and publicly committed to change. But month on month, despite my conscious efforts and commitment, in moments of weakness or temptation, I would fall back to the same old behaviour. The drives that cause behaviour—sense of self-identity, insecurities, belief system—are all so deeply rooted in the subconscious that they keep surfacing repeatedly. And I kept asking myself, 'Am I fake, in that I made a commitment and am not able to live up to it?' This book—and the concept of 'brain as a team of rivals' helped me understand the enormity of the behavioural change challenge, and hopefully with this wisdom, this too shall pass. No wonder Carl Jung used to say, 'In each of us there is another whom we do not know!'

The ability to effect a sustained change is one problem as we saw above. The other end of the spectrum, when we do change, is a tendency to overcorrect. Behaviour change is like a pendulum—it oscillates to each extreme for some time before settling down to the middle.

The beauty of it all is that we don't have to ace every aspect of our game. Showing a bit of vulnerability in front of our team and selectively sharing our journey towards improvement can be a game changer. The environment becomes more accommodative of some of our flaws when they see sincere effort. Also, people succeed because of their strengths, so we can survive with some weaknesses too. We just need to ensure our weaknesses do not become serious stumbling blocks or derailers. In other words, we don't need to ace our weaknesses, just improve them to a working level. Once we know our weak areas, we can also complement ourselves with people under and around us who have that skill set.

Beyond the professional advantages of improving on these core skills, there is a wider impact as well. These are largely behavioural, and once mastered, help us become a better person. If we can practise more self-awareness, control our emotions more, collaborate more, deliver on priorities more or rejuvenate more, our personal lives will improve. Our significant relationships beyond work—family and friends—will become stronger too. The best compliment I got after becoming a *7*

*Habits* trainer was from my wife. She said I have started listening and understanding her more.

It was a small sentence with a huge impact, and I have seen this echoed in participants of the *Timeless Skills* workshop. They tell us how these principles have transformed their lives outside of work—spouses, children, friends all notice and appreciate the positive change.

So, let us begin this journey—not just to be better professionals but to become better people.

# Summary

- Most skills needed for career advancement are behavioural and not purely cognitive. Hence, they can't simply be learnt in a classroom.
- Changing attitude (tendency to behave in a particular way) and behaviour is difficult but is achievable.
- Attitude is influenced by past experiences which shape our mindset. To change, we must first change our mindset.
- Classroom training is helpful, but on its own, it's not enough for sustained behaviour change. Awareness, deep motivation, constant practise and feedback are essential for behavioural change.
- Stress can bring out ingrained tendencies and impact overall behaviour. Behaviour change itself swings between extremes.
- Improvement doesn't require perfection; acknowledging and working on weaknesses is a good start.
- Becoming a better person positively impacts all aspects of life, including relationships with family and friends.

## Food for Thought: Self-Assessment

1.  If I were to create a fictional character based on my own attitude and behavioural tendencies, what beliefs and mindsets would this character possess?

2.  Reflecting on my own personality and on the story of the CEO who struggled with public outbursts due to a deeply ingrained mindset, can any deep-rooted mindset or paradigm be identified that may be influencing unhelpful behaviour or attitude? How can it be challenged to improve?

3.  What unhelpful behaviour have I been trying to change, but keeps returning? If a trigger event or experience were designed to catalyze a significant mindset shift, what would it look like? How could this experience lead to lasting behavioural change?

4.  Have I ever leaned too heavily on a particular strength to the point where it became a limitation? Tending to swing between extremes rather than finding a balanced middle ground, how can greater stability and moderation be achieved in these areas?

5.   Reflecting on the impact of one's behaviour on relationships beyond the workplace, how could improving my core behavioural skills such as self-awareness, emotional control, collaboration and prioritization enhance personal life and connections with others?

6.   If I were participating in a group discussion focused on the intersection of neuroscience and behaviour change, what experiences from my own life could be shared? What personal revelations have been gained in this regard?

# Part 2| Seven Timeless Skills

## Self-Management

'I have lived on the lip of insanity, wanting to know reasons, knocking on a door. It opens. I have been knocking from the inside'—**Rumi, thirteenth century Sufi mystical poet**

'Until you make the unconscious conscious, it will direct your life and you will call it fate'—**Carl Jung, founder of analytical psychology, best known for his work *Memories, Dreams, Reflections***

Someone once said that if management is an art, the artist's true tool is the self. How can we hope to guide others without first refining ourselves?

One of my favourite stories is that of a perturbed mother who is concerned about her son's unhealthy habit of eating too much sugar. Since her son revered Gandhi, she walks miles with her son to see Gandhi and requests the Mahatma to dissuade her son from this unhealthy habit. Gandhi takes one look at her boy and asks them both to return after two weeks. The mother is disappointed, but nevertheless makes the same arduous journey with her son again. However, this time, Gandhi takes the son aside and has a little discussion with him. The son, with his eyes brimming with tears, makes a solemn commitment to forsake his habit.

The mother is overjoyed but puzzled. She asks Gandhi why the same message couldn't have been delivered in the first visit. Gandhi remarks, 'You don't understand, at that time, even I was consuming too much sugar.' So, the saint that he was, he first stopped eating sugar himself and only then earned the moral right to correct the son.

Gandhi's life philosophy was all about first controlling his own urges—whether through fasting up to twenty-one days, only speaking the truth, living a life of utmost simplicity or even engaging in his more controversial experiments with celibacy. He believed that only when we first conquer ourselves, can we think of influencing others.

This journey of self conquest spans three distinct areas:[1]

## Self-Awareness

From Plato's time, sages have guided us to *Know Thyself.* And yet, although 95 per cent of people think they are self-aware, only 10 to 15 per cent actually are.[2]

First, we must know and accept our strengths and our weaknesses because only then can we know what to leverage and where to seek help. As the oracle of Omaha, Warren Buffet, (for many years the world's richest man) very wisely said, 'You have to stick within what I call your circle of competence. You have to know what you understand and what you don't understand. It's not terribly important how big the circle is. But it's terribly important that you know where the perimeter is.'

360-degree feedback—where managers, peers and subordinates all join us in assessing our strengths and weaknesses—is a great way to gain this awareness. Successful people love to get clear actionable feedback, so they know where to improve. I have implemented this simple technique for myself and for my teams in every single leadership role I have had. Unfortunately, many people get defensive when confronted with adverse feedback and tend to overrate their own abilities, thus ending up not improving. In most 360 reports, people's assessment of their own selves was at least 20-30% higher than how their peers perceived them.

Beyond knowing our strengths and weaknesses, self-awareness also means recognizing our insecurities and fears. Many fast risers, while brilliant in their work, suffer from inherent self-doubt and low self-esteem which hinders them from completely enjoying their success.

I was reading *Lean In*, Sheryl Sandberg's autobiography. As the former COO of Facebook and one of the world's highest paid executives, her achievements are remarkable—Harvard, McKinsey, Google, Facebook, bestselling author. But what truly resonated with me was her candid admission: 'Every time I was called on in class, I was sure that I was about to embarrass myself . . . This phenomenon of capable people being plagued by self-doubt has a name—the imposter syndrome . . . I still have days when I feel like a fraud.'[3]

Often this self-doubt manifests itself as a temptation to be liked, to please others. Sheryl recounted the first message she got from Facebook founder Mark Zukerberg: 'One of the things he told me was that the desire to be liked by everyone would hold me back. He said that when you want to change things, you can't please everyone. If you do please everyone, you aren't making enough progress.'

I have personally grappled with both self-imposed anxiety and a strong desire to stay in others' good graces. When Cipla provided me with a coach, he quickly recognized this pattern and introduced me to the work of psychologist Albert Ellis (often considered one of the top three psychotherapists alongside Carl Rogers and Sigmund Freud). Ellis theorized that negative emotions stem from mistaken beliefs about ourselves, others and the world.

For me and for many young achievers this mistaken belief was: 'I absolutely MUST perform well to win the approval of others. If I fail, that is awful and it will prove that I am an incompetent person, who will probably often fail.'

This belief works fine till all is going well, and, in fact, helps in our achievement drive. But when faced with adversity or situations outside our control, holding this belief tends to contribute to feelings of anxiety, panic, depression, despair and worthlessness.

Finally, self-awareness also tells us what we can control and what we can't, and hence where to focus our energy. The wise stoic philosopher Epictetus of Greece started the ruminations on those things in our power (*prohairetic* things) and those things not in our power (*aprohairetic* things): 'Happiness and freedom begin with a clear understanding of one principle: Some things are within our power, while others are not. That alone is in our power, which is our own work; and in this class are our opinions, impulses, desires, and aversions. On the contrary, what is not in our power are our bodies, possessions, glory, and power. We have no power over external things, and the good that ought to be the object of our earnest pursuit, is to be found only within ourselves.'

While a lot has changed in our world over these 2000 years, the essential wisdom of good living has not. Successful people focus their energy on what they can control, though they may still have opinions on—and be influenced by—external factors. But they don't waste too much energy or effort on them. They learn to adapt to things truly outside their control, so they can make a real difference in what they can control.

I was intrigued by the World Happiness Survey rankings where the Nordic countries (Norway, Sweden, Denmark, Iceland) consistently came out on top.[4] So, my family and I planned an extended trip there, eager to learn first-hand what makes these countries so resiliently happy, despite their cold, dark and often gloomy climate. When we asked locals about their secret to happiness, pat came the reply, 'There is no bad weather, only bad clothes.'

We can fret and chafe about the weather, or the endless and exhausting traffic that makes us late for meetings, or the long queues at the cashier of the grocery store (all of which we have little to no control over).

Or

We can focus on what is truly within our hands, having the right outlook to deal with the situation. Wearing better clothes that can withstand the weather or finding life hacks to do when stuck in traffic. This is a larger philosophy of living: Understand that of all things that we are concerned about, there is a very small subset of things that are within our control. Focus our energy on what is within our control instead of wasting it on what we can't change.

I experienced this first-hand when I was transferred to Mumbai. Every day, my colleagues and I would brace the infamous Mumbai traffic for hours, surrounded by heavy congestion, honking vehicles, thick clouds of exhaust, relentless humidity and then pot-holed roads. The drain on emotions, time and health is so immense that Elon Musk called traffic a 'soul destroying experience.' For the first few weeks, I kept venting out my frustration like everybody else. And then, inspired by the concept of the circle of control, I decided to focus on what was in my power. I moved to an apartment close to my office, sold my car and started walking every day to work, a total of twelve minutes each way. The traffic situation remained the same, but I started saving two hours of time a day, and much more on energy.

Another example of not fretting over things beyond our power is in not overmanaging our careers. While it is good to be ambitious, sometimes we put a very high premium on what we want *and* by when we want it. During my campus placement season at IIM Lucknow, I was a bit disappointed by the absence of investment banking and consulting recruiters. But then, just when I joined P&G, they gave me a very lucrative expatriate posting in Japan. Why me? Out of sheer luck. I just happened to be the only returning intern in finance, and the finance analyst in Japan had just resigned requiring an urgent replacement. Since that 'lucky break' foreign posting, my career took an international turn and now I have lived and worked in six countries. I often ruminate that my first break had as much to do with luck as hard work. On the days when my teenage daughter comes home frustrated, I tell her: Life is only 50 per cent fair. The good news is that it is as fair to you as it will be unfair, and in the long run, these tend to even out. So just focus on your circle of control and calmly accept things outside it.

This concept played out once again in my career. I was posted to Philippines as the head of general ledger accounting in what was one of the first Knowledge Process Outsourcing (KPO) centres in Asia. As a card holding member of the MBA community, I was a bit hesitant to take on what was primarily an accounting role, ensuring accurate and timely bookkeeping of accounts for twenty countries in Asia. But my mentor gave me a sage advice: If you strategically think about being a CFO one day, there is no chance you can do it without a deep knowledge of accounting. Take this time to get all the knowledge available in the whole wide world on core finance. I took it as a challenge and read extensively about accounting rules, so much so that I started getting invites to deliver lectures in the Continuing Professional Education (CPE) programmes of Chartered Professional Accountants (CPAs), similar to Indian chartered accountants. And very soon did become CFO of a large business.

Of course, maturity demands we also know the right balance between these two bookends: Accepting things versus trying to change them. If we start bowing down to every challenge saying it is not in our power to control it, we will become defeatist and won't go very far. To resolve this dilemma, one may find the serenity prayer below exceptionally wise:

> *Lord, give me the courage to change the things I can,*
> *The serenity to accept the things I can't,*
> *And the wisdom to know the difference.*

So, to sum up, self-awareness is about knowing our strengths, weaknesses, insecurities, fears and anxieties. It is also about controlling the controllables, knowing what is within our control and what is beyond, so that we can focus our energy on what we can influence. This helps in life and career.

## Self-Control

> 'No one can make you jealous, angry, vengeful, or greedy—unless you let him'—**Napoleon Hill, author of *Think and Grow Rich*, the highest selling self-help book of all time**

'The secret of success is learning how to use pain and pleasure instead of having pain and pleasure use you. If you do that, you're in control of your life. If you don't, life controls you'— **Tony Robbins, bestselling author of _Unlimited Power and Awaken the Giant Within_**

An old Native American was teaching his grandson about life.

'A fight is going on inside all of us,' he said to the boy. 'It is a terrible fight and it is between two wolves. One is evil— anger, jealousy, regret, greed, arrogance, self-pity, inferiority, lies, superiority and ego.'

He continued, 'The other is good—joy, peace, love, hope, serenity, humility, kindness, empathy, generosity and truth.'

The grandson asked, 'Which wolf will win?'

The old man simply replied, 'The one you feed.'

In my _Timeless Skills_ class, a participant dryly remarked: 'I want to change, I am committed to improve. But what can I do? My spouse is just so difficult that I cannot help but react. Can you not offer this training to her!'

This happens a lot. We blame our lack of self-control to external environment and outside influence. And paint ourselves as innocent victims who didn't really have freedom to choose a response. The external stimulus—say from a bickering boss or colleagues or spouse—was just too powerful not to impulsively react. The problem with this approach, however, is that it takes away our freedom of choice. In our attempt to feel more in control (by faulting others for our experience), we strip ourselves of our own power to self regulate. That power is lost the moment we become dependent on other people or things to make us feel a certain way. In reality, we can decide which emotion to feed.

And so, I gently guide my students to the classic tribute to hope, _Man's Search for Meaning_, by Professor Viktor Frankl.

For those unaware of what actually happened in the holocaust in the Second World War, fifteen million people, including two-thirds of the entire Jewish population of Europe, were murdered. Viktor Frankl, a Jew, lived through those horrendous concentration camps, where he and others were subjected to the worst forms of torture and inhuman behaviour probably known to mankind. While his entire family, including his pregnant wife, perished, he came out alive to tell this story.

In the horrific situation inside the holocaust concentration camps, he saw most people break down emotionally, but some others retained their calm and inner strength, despite the triggers being the same for everyone. In the same adverse situation, while most collapsed, some continued to walk through the huts comforting others, giving away their last piece of bread. Which is why he makes his famous statement, 'Everything can be taken from a man but one thing: the last of the human freedoms— to choose one's attitude in any given set of circumstances . . . between the stimulus and response, there is a space. And in that space lies our freedom and power to choose our responses.'[5]

I visited Frankl's Museum in Vienna and came back even more convinced: Circumstances can powerfully influence us, tempt us to behave in a particular way. But they cannot decide our response. We alone have the power to choose our response.

In many ways this *ability to choose our response* is the essence of what makes us human. I did a snake handling course in Cape Town where, to earn the coveted certificate, we had to catch a non-sedated, venomous cobra by the tail. While it sounds dangerous, once we learnt the nature of the reptile, it was much easier (though obviously NOT recommended without expert guidance). Just stand in front of the cobra outside its striking range, usually a distance of 3 feet, and stay still without making any movement. Like clockwork, when it sees the threat subside, it will put its hood down and start moving away from you. And then you carefully grab it by the tail. All Cape cobras will behave very similarly. They have not yet evolved to have a consciousness which allows them to choose their individual response.

If we start reacting to every trigger automatically, we will be no better than reptiles. We will end up consenting to others making our lives miserable.

Author Stephen Covey described what he called the 90/ 10 principle.[6] Ten per cent of life is made up of what happens to us. Ninety per cent of life is shaped by how we react. We really have no control over 10 per cent of what happens to us. But the real outcome of our lives, the 90 per cent, is our own doing. In his class, he had us do a simple exercise: Imagine our daughter spills ketchup on our shirt just as we're about to leave for work. How do we react? Many of us, hand on heart, would scold the kid, lose our calm, perhaps even snap at our spouse as she tries to justify the kid's action. Then, drive to work, our mood soured, anxious about being late for an important meeting. Every red light would feel like a personal attack, and by the time we arrive at the office, we exhibit anything but the calm, smiling persona needed to shine in the meeting. After the boss rubs in our tardiness, the whole day we remain sullen, complaining to everyone, and flaring up at slight provocations. In the evening, when we return home, we meet the wife and kid who we left upset before leaving, and we vent about how unjust life is. The point is that the real 'injustice' to us—the five-minute delay due to the ketchup spill—was perhaps outside our control. But the wastage of the entire day—the frustration, the anger, the shouting, the rush—was all our chosen reaction to what happened to us. The 90/ 10 principle illustrated.

And hence, wise people learn to self regulate. The late Richard Carlson of *Don't Sweat The Small Stuff* series of books fame, used to ponder: If we step back and really think about it, much of what bugs us on a day-to-day basis is actually the 'small stuff'—tiffs within office or home, traffic problems, difficult deadlines, wasteful meetings, office bureaucracy, requests not being answered, stinker emails, demanding bosses, an assumed rat race, etc. The real problems of life—job layoffs, theft or violence—are really few and far between. Indeed, it's all those little hassles that tend to drive us crazy.[7] And therefore, because there is so much 'small stuff' to deal with at work, there is a direct correlation between the way we handle small stuff and our overall effectiveness at work. If only we can learn to treat the smaller hassles with more perspective, wisdom, patience and with a better sense of humour, we will begin to bring out the best in ourselves.

Self control has been taught from time immemorial even by our Indian sages. My favourite Upanishad (also called *Vedanta*, literally the highest point of our ancient Vedas), *Kathoupanishad*, starts with explaining the difference between *shreyas* and *preyas*. The wise discriminate between what is really good (shreyas) vs what feels merely pleasant at that moment (preyas). There are a lot of temptations around us which may provide instant pleasure but are harmful in the long run, and so the wise man prefers what is truly good over what is just momentarily tempting. The text gives the analogy of the chariot which goes on a straight path only if we rein in the horses. (Intriguingly, a very similar analogy of the charioteer was taught by Plato too in 'Phaedrus'.)

How do we know when we have mastered this self-control? Daniel Goleman puts the acid test: 'The signs of emotional self-regulation are easy to see: a propensity for reflection and thoughtfulness; comfort with ambiguity and change; and integrity—an ability to say no to impulsive urges.'[8]

## Self-Motivation

Recently, when my batchmates met for the twenty-fifth reunion of our engineering college, someone remarked that those who were relatively successful today led a very active life at campus. It could be trying to be academically in the top 20 per cent of the batch, writing technical papers, speaking in conferences, doing industry live projects, leading clubs, participating in extra curriculars and so on. These colleagues were full of passion and energy. They sought out challenges, excelled at going above and beyond and took pride in getting things done.

In behavioural terms, their locus of control was internal. For such people, delivering great results is not primarily because of an external reward, but primarily because of an inner desire for achievement. They are proactive, meaning they do before they are asked to do.

One of my favourite psychology theories is nAch or Need for Achievement,[9] made famous by the psychologist David McClelland[10] (from Harvard and Yale, one of the fifteen most cited psychologists of all time): 'Intense, prolonged and repeated efforts to accomplish something difficult, to work with singleness of purpose towards a high and distant goal, and to have the determination to win.' In short, a person's innate drive to achieve something significant.

For such people:

1. Achievement is more important than material or financial reward. It gives greater personal satisfaction than receiving praise or recognition. In fact, successful people are not primarily after money, but after achievement.

2. Financial reward may be regarded as one measure of success, but not an end in itself. Security is not the prime motivator, nor is status.

3. Feedback (reliable, quantifiable and factual) is essential because it enables measurement of success and helps improve.

I had a driver, Gladwin Segalo, in Cape Town. He had big dreams and kept asking me what he could do to improve. Coming from a slum, he had a lot to be angry about,[11] but he chose to focus on breaking the cycle of poverty and becoming a role model for his community. Energized by his self-motivation, I shared multiple leadership books with him. And in our time together in the car, we discussed management and success themes. He soaked in everything, driven by a huge inner energy despite all the drag of his everyday existence. I moved to a different country, but we kept exchanging letters. Recently, he told me how he joined an operations firm and worked his way up from call taker to team leader to operations manager—a dream designation given where he came from.

The opposite phenomenon that corroborates this theory is known as the Overjustification Effect.[12] It occurs when external rewards (like recognition and accolades) become the primary focus. This dilutes one's original internal motivation for the activity. Individuals get accustomed to that instant dopamine boost afforded by the validation associated with external rewards, forgetting the initial enjoyment they once found in the activity even without any external gratification. And since all glory is fleeting, such external cues are unable to sustain motivation.

People who are self-motivated also show high levels of resilience, a critical quality especially after COVID. The pandemic left the world in a chaotic state of flux. Against the unprecedented challenges of the pandemic—from economic downturns to social isolation—those with a resilient mindset were better equipped to bounce back, finding the courage to rise again after failure.

When I became a young general manager, we had a bad financial quarter. Unaccustomed to underperformance or failure, I naturally carried a look of dejection, disappointed in myself for letting the team down. Our CEO gave me some good advice: 'Chin up, put a smile on the face and get ready for the next quarter.' As a business head, we will have good and bad quarters, but the team will start having existential doubts if their leader is down. Take some time to recover but after that come back recharged.

In one of our monthly 'lunch and learn' sessions, I had invited a former president of a Fortune 50 company. He recounted this episode from his early years: 'My new manager said you are not as good as everybody says you are and maybe you should leave. And, instead of being offended, I asked for six months to prove myself. Long story short, this same manager promoted me and sent me abroad as an expat.'

One of the earliest pieces of advice I received was to develop a thick skin and not sweat the small stuff. Self-motivated individuals tend to exhibit high levels of positivity and optimism, and Elon Musk is a prime example of this mindset. When he set his sights on private space exploration, Musk travelled to Russia with the goal of purchasing a rocket. The military seller mocked him, questioning how a young 'nerd' could even think of buying a rocket. To make matters worse, he spat on his shoes. Rather than being discouraged, Musk returned even more determined and began designing his own rocket. In fact, during the flight home, he started sketching out his plans for a new spacecraft. His first attempt, Falcon 1, failed during its launch. But Musk didn't give up. The second and third launches also ended in failure. It wasn't until the fourth attempt that Falcon 1 successfully reached orbit, becoming the world's first privately funded rocket, catapulting Musk to global fame.

I tend to become protective of my daughters. As caring parents, we want to shield them from life's problems. But in doing so, we forget that the very struggles we try to protect them from are the ones that shaped our own character. Take Jensen Huang, the CEO of Nvidia, for example. He started as a dishwasher and now has a net worth of USD 80 billion. He told Stanford students that success is earned through suffering: 'I wish upon you ample doses of pain and suffering . . . greatness comes from character and character isn't formed out of smart people, it is formed out of people who suffered.'

This is resilience—bouncing back even in the face of adversity. The opposite of resilience is being overly sensitive, letting anxiety or nervousness take over after every setback. It's about staying grounded, even when things don't go as planned. So, as the lyrics of Rema's famous song say so beautifully, 'Baby calm down, calm down.'

# Summary

- Successful people, before they try to change the world, learn how to manage themselves.
- Self-management involves three key areas: self-awareness, self-control and self-motivation.
- Self-awareness means knowing our strengths, weaknesses, fears and insecurities. It also involves understanding what we can control and therefore where to focus our energy.
- Self-control involves choosing our responses to external stimuli rather than reacting impulsively.
- Self-motivation entails pursuing goals for personal satisfaction rather than external rewards. Resilience and positivity are essential traits of self-motivated individuals.
- Keep smiling. It is not worth it to fret the small stuff. And in the end, it is all small stuff.

## Food for Thought: Self-Assessment

1. What are my deepest insecurities? What are the thoughts that sometimes keep me from sleeping or wake me up in the middle of the night?

2. What are my hot buttons—situations where reactions tend to be disproportionate to the initial trigger? What causes emotional and impulsive responses instead of calm and logical ones?

3. Recall personal experiences of self-doubt or imposter syndrome. What underlying beliefs or narratives about myself contributed to these feelings? How can these beliefs be challenged and reframed to build greater self-confidence?

4. Reflect on the idea of focusing on the circle of control. Do I tend to expend energy on things outside my control? How can focus be shifted to the sphere of influence instead?

5. In what ways do I allow external validation or rewards to influence motivation and fulfillment? Is true self-motivation present?

6.  When faced with the last serious setback, did I feel discouraged or disheartened? Are there days when others have noticed a sullen or grumpy demeanor?

# 4

# Clarity

'I suspect that they put Socrates to death because there is something terribly unattractive, alienating, and nonhuman in thinking with too much clarity'—**Nassim Taleb, author of *The Black Swan***

'Clear thinking is more valuable than mere intelligence... Simplifying complex ideas for easy understanding shows deep knowledge'—**Naval Ravikant, founder, USD 4 billion Angel List**

My mother has been a doctor all her life. Seeing her in the clinic, I have always marvelled at how good doctors spend inordinate time trying to understand and decipher all the symptoms of the patient. They cut through the noise to identify the real symptom, ensuring the right diagnosis before beginning treatment. A fever can mean so many things, mostly benign (like common flu) but sometimes critical (like some forms of cancer). A headache is usually harmless, say due to stress, but, in rare cases, could also be a secondary sign of an underlying brain bleed. Inexperienced doctors misread symptoms and start solving a non-existent problem. My father was ill and got misdiagnosed with tuberculosis. The unnecessary treatment worsened his condition. Thankfully, a skilled doctor later identified the correct illness, and with the right treatment, my father was able to recover quickly.

## A. Identifying the (Real) Problem

This clear-thinking ability is gold: Identifying the real issue amongst all the noise—to see all data points and find the common denominator. In our MBA course, in marketing cases, we spent more than half the class time just on problem identification. If we can clearly write the real problem statement, then using known tools to solve it is the easier piece. It sounds straightforward, right? However, in real life—with static interference from other symptoms, information overload, our own biases, limited time, thinking flaws, multiple hypotheses— the problem is that the (identified) problem is usually not the (real) problem. No wonder, consulting companies charge a bomb to tell us our problem statement which they extract after talking to our teams.

I joined Procter & Gamble (P&G) and was the project leader for a new launch. Sales in the initial months were subpar, prompting the cross-functional team to gather, analyse what went wrong, and take corrective action.

- The marketing person felt product awareness was still low and asked for more advertising money to bring sales back on track.
- The consumer insights person thought trial was low and wanted to increase trial by offering samples and reducing price.

- The sales guy suggested our distribution reach was the issue and asked for more money to increase the pull from stockists.
- The finance person, on the other hand, recommended cutting spending to maintain profit commitment since sales were already low.

Each of these suggestions sounded logical but could also be flowing from inherent biases of the functional team. Thankfully, P&G followed a very data-based approach, and we compared each of the individual sales drivers (awareness, trial, repeat, consumption, distribution etc.) with the original assumption before launch. We found that while awareness, trial and distribution hadn't peaked, they weren't significantly off from the original goal-setter assumptions.

The main issue was this: The repeat rate (per cent of first time trialists coming back to buy the brand again) was significantly lower (<10 per cent) than original assumptions (>30 per cent). To understand why this was happening, we did a small consumer research survey with trialists who had not repeated. Their main complaint was in the product quality itself, with the flavour we had used. So, we went back to R&D, got the issue fixed and then sales picked up too.

This little anecdote brings out a few insights:

- In business and life, there will rarely be one issue—multiple symptoms (each real) will cloud our judgement.
- But most of these will be adjacent; there will only be one or two prime causes.
- If we don't understand and attack the core issue, we will end up spending good money behind bad money. The problem will not go away.

- Even intelligent people will tend to respond from their biases and focus on side issues, instead of the main issue.
- There is a scientific method to keep questioning and probing and challenging till we can separate incorrect hypotheses from the real deal.
- Hard data can separate facts from mere opinion. One of my managers used to say, 'In God we trust. Everyone else brings data!'

No wonder one of the skills P&G looked at while hiring was problem-solving ability—the raw ability to look at data, extract insights, separate the symptom from the real issue and make an action plan. I have failed each time I tried to solve a problem by simply throwing more money or people, instead of clearly identifying the root cause.

This problem-solving ability is not just useful in business, but also, and perhaps more so, in life. The ability to take rational, well thought out decisions instead of getting swayed by emotions; the patience to sift through surface symptoms and keep probing till we see unblemished truth; the ability to calmly evaluate multiple scenarios before zooming into what makes most sense . . . in a sense, seeing farther and clearer than others. Decision-making—whether choice of project in corporate, choice of career, choice of a spouse, or choice of a house—becomes simpler once we are clear-headed.

## B. Mastering Thinking Fallacies

In problem-solving, much like a sumptuous buffet, choosing wisely is key. Just as we pick—or at any rate should pick—nutritious food over tempting treats for our well-being, identifying the core problem amidst distractions is vital for success. Prioritizing substance over allure leads to effective decisions.

Decisions usually have to be made with vague, incomplete and conflicting information. What may appear rational superficially may, on closer inspection, be biased or erroneous.

. Let me recount a real example from the hallowed world of mergers and acquisitions (M&A). In 2005, P&G decided to buy Gillette in what would be one of the world's largest acquisitions and creating the world's largest consumer products enterprise. The former had a largely female buyer base while the latter was the leading men's grooming company. So, management felt there could be significant synergies. I was in M&A and rather academically inclined. I wanted to check what the gurus of valuation had to say about the 'fair' price that P&G should pay to acquire Gillette. Aswath Damodaran, the famous Stern valuation professor (and also my inspiration for choosing finance), suggested on his famous blog that P&G should pay USD 25 billion and no more. While Joel Stern (the founder of Economic Value Added and founder of Stern Stewart company) suggested to me in a conference that the maximum purchase price should be USD 42 billion. But Gillette was a well performing listed company and its market capitalization was already USD 40–45 billion, so unless a buyer gave a substantial premium, why would their current shareholders sell the company?

When P&G's own finance department did the same valuation, they decided to pay USD 57 billion to buy Gillette, a premium of 18 per cent over Gillette's then share price.

Which valuation was correct? All three were based largely on similar publicly available information since both buyer and seller were listed on the US stock exchange.

In retrospect, the P&G–Gillette acquisition is regarded as one of the best acquisitions in the consumer goods sector, creating significant long-term value for both shareholders. So perhaps the offered valuation was reasonable after all. But that is not the main takeaway here.

The point is that three intelligent people, using similar public data, arrived at valuations that differed by billions. Numbers are supposed to be the objective truth, and yet are anything but.[1] The accounting person tends to make conservative assumptions while the commercial person may make aggressive ones. Therefore, the numbers can swing significantly, allowing both sides to 'justify' their stand. Based on such valuations, crucial buy vs not-to-buy decisions are made. Hence, the dry remark that decisions are first made 'emotionally' and then justified rationally with numbers.

There are many examples of preconceived biases and errors in judgement clouding objective decision making. In fact, one of my favourite books, *Art Of Thinking Clearly* by Rolf Dobelli, suggests there could be many flaws in our thinking process itself and elaborates ninety-nine such flaws.[2] Some of the more common ones—from the book and beyond—are listed here:

**Fooled by Successes:** As a professional investor, I often get tempted to invest in a start-up, inspired by India's many unicorn success stories. But a more sober analysis suggests that only a very small fraction of all start-ups reach that milestone, and the more likely scenario for most investments is that they will not cross the finish line.

**Cause vs Effect:** We see handsome and beautiful models who sell cosmetics, and we buy the goods, hoping the purchase will make us look like them. But these models were born attractive and chosen for advertising because of their existing features, not the other way around. Beauty is usually a factor for selection and not the result.

**Sunk Cost Fallacy:** If we have already invested a lot of time, money or energy in something, that itself becomes a reason to carry on, even if everyone around us knows we are 'dealing with a lost cause.' We have all seen marketing people continue to ask for more investment, when all around the table know the launch was a failure.

**Confirmation Bias:** The 'mother of all misconceptions . . . tendency to interpret new information so that it becomes compatible with our existing theories and beliefs . . . we filter out any new information that contradicts our existing views.' We are on a weight loss diet; when we lose weight, we pat ourselves on the back but when we gain, we take it as normal fluctuation. This continues for months, and we tell everyone our diet is working while our weight remains constant.

**Contrast Effect:** Humans have difficulty with absolute judgements and hence judge something to be beautiful, expensive or good if we have something relatively ugly, cheap or not good in front of us. All upgrade options exploit this. Compared to a Rs 20 lakhs price tag on a car, Rs 30,000 leather seats sound like a pittance and people go for this additional purchase.

**Causation vs Correlation:** The joke was that in a small city, sales of ice-cream and cases of theft were increasing together, an unmistakable correlation. But why was this happening? After a while, the real cause was understood—summers. With frequent power cuts, people were sleeping in their open terrace at night, making it easier for thieves to come in. And yes, they were also consuming more ice-cream.

We could go on . . . the skill of clarity requires us to understand the flaws in our thinking and therefore obviate their influence in actual decisions.

## C. Understanding How Things 'Really' Work

Understanding how exactly the world operates requires us to think beyond armchair theory and desk research and imbibe the real world in the pursuit of truth. One of my B-school professors used to say successful people exhibit CCCF—Conceptual Clarity and Contextual Familiarity. The first—clarity—is the focus of this chapter. The second—knowing the context deeply—is what we cover in this section.

Anyone who has been to a hill station would know how difficult it is to find our path amidst all the fog. We know there is a right path, but our vision is murky because of the fog. What is needed is a guiding light to help us see through the haze, a clarity that maps the path in our head helping us reach the right destination. Without this clarity, we will remain lost.

In my first role as an analyst in P&G's beauty care business, I quickly realized that our colour cosmetics segment (lipstick, mascara, etc.—a role my wife loved, especially for the free cosmetics) had a fundamental business model issue: too many shades, excessive inventory, frequent write-offs with changing fashion seasons, and, as a result, constant losses. So, I boldly recommended to our CEO that we should shut the segment down. He smiled and asked me to spend the next two weeks at the department store, seeing first-hand how sales were made. Once there, the penny dropped—I saw how colour cosmetics were actually drawing most of the footfalls to our counter, allowing our beauty counsellors to cross-sell highly profitable skincare products. Later, I read about McDonald's model of selling their base cheeseburger at minimal profits but making significant profit on chips and cola that most customers bought along with the burger. So, while my technical ability (Microsoft Excel analytics in this case) was impeccable, my thinking was still flawed since I didn't know how the world actually operated.

A slight digression: While 'wicked problems' don't have an easy solution, they can still have an easy narrative. Think of how politicians win elections. Across different nations, political leaders promise the moon to naïve voters: there is poverty, so if voted to power, they will dole out, say, free food. But hard economics rarely offers a free lunch.

Even well-intentioned policies, if not thought through clearly, have unintended consequences, making the medicine worse than the malady. In the example of distributing free food to reduce poverty, funding such a big largesse would require charging higher taxes (and hence lower money in circulation, thereby impeding growth and hence employment) or printing more notes (leading to inflation and general increase in prices of all goods) or reducing spending in other priority sectors (like health and education, which means the same poor will spend more money on private clinics and coaching classes). Beyond these fundamental questions is the issue of execution on the ground in a large country (e.g. free grains could lead to the creation of a black market where middlemen or even the poor sell the same grains for a profit). Unless we have clarity on all these aspects and incorporate them in policymaking, real impact will keep eluding us. We will make grandiose plans, but they will fall flat.

Case in point: India launched the National Food Security Act in 2011 with a very noble intent: 'About two thirds of the population will be entitled to receive subsidized food grains... in a country where almost 40 per cent of children are undernourished.' And yet, even after a decade of executing this policy, India's rank in Global Hunger Index continues to remain extremely low: fifty-five out of seventy-six countries in 2014 and now 111 out of 125 countries in 2023.[3]

Understanding the context and how the world really operates helps us in all facets of life, including hiring. One of my former company's promoter often used to say, 'I don't like putting a square peg in a round hole.' The individual is great but stuck in a wrong role that does not fully leverage his strengths. Each role demands different qualities: One role may require a hard-nosed, even ruthless cost cutter. Another may require inspiring a large team with vision, support and genuine care. *Ceteris Paribus*, the same individual, with the same skill set, may or may not succeed in both these roles because the contexts are different. So, clear thinking also helps decide where we fit in.

## D. What Exactly Is Our Right to Win?

'Right to Win' in business identifies what sets us apart and why we will succeed despite competition.

Whenever we evaluate a new project while trying to ascertain whether or not it will succeed, we look at: What really is our Right to Win. Why exactly will we succeed when there will be others who will also see the same opportunity and put in similar effort?

In B-school, we used to study the case of Southwest Airlines which became one of the earliest success stories in low-cost carriers. It developed its entire ecosystem around low cost— bought small planes; used smaller, cheaper airports outside main city; reduced service offering; chose routes connecting tier-2 cities and so on. It was difficult for the incumbents—with their larger airplanes and operations in expensive cities—to match Southwest's cost offering.[4]

In any pursuit—be it business, career or even love—there is a foundational question to ask: What is my Right to Win? For a student at campus placements, it is important to question, why would they choose me? What are my standout strengths? What sets me apart from the other hundred candidates? For a lover, the question shifts: What makes me the one? How am I a better choice for her than her other suitors? Identifying this 'Right to Win' forces us to look inward, uncovering what makes us not just capable, but irresistible, and undeniably the best choice.

## E. Conception Before Execution

I pursued an engineering degree before my MBA. Our friends in the civil department, even before laying the first brick, would get a clear conception of the end state in their head. Which material would withstand the rain and soil, what tensile strength would support the height, what thickness would keep it warm inside and so on. The design is ready, crystal clear, before execution begins. The clearer the conception, the vision, the plan, the clearer will be the execution. Same goes with all our endeavours. Thinking right must precede acting right. Failed businesses are still run by intelligent, hard-working people. But somewhere they were lacking clarity on the most crucial things. No wonder the genius of Einstein said that we cannot solve our problems with the same thinking we used when we created them. Hence, this chapter centres clarity as a core success skill in itself. In fact, I read somewhere that clear thinking ability is perhaps a bigger compliment than say intelligence or hard work. Sifting through all the noise, identifying the real issues at hand, being aware of our own thinking flaws, understanding how the world truly operates. Knowing the few things, if focussed on intensely, that will lead to great results.

Some of this comes with experience. Just as a guitarist learns to navigate the fretboard with ease, individuals gain clarity and confidence in their pursuits through practise. Experience— good or bad—gives perspective and allows us to reach the root problem quickly. There is a much-shared meme on how a plumber keeps looking at a leak and then fixes it immediately. When he charges a big bill, the customer complains how he could charge so much for just five minutes of work. He retorts, 'I charge you for 10 years of experience.'

In my own case, a few months into the CEO role, the big question I asked myself was: What exactly is the CEO's role? There was a humbling realization that the daily rigamarole of business will happen with or without me. Sales team will still get orders, operations team will still fulfil those orders. So, what was my unique contribution? Unless I can conceptualize this *raison d'etre* clearly, how will I create a legacy?

In my case, I felt the role is to make the business move in unthinkable ways. Large corporates need to learn from Private Equity or Venture Capital fund's ability to scale businesses fast. Bold ambition, frugal thinking, quick decision making, no nonsense focus on KRAs and aligning interests. Hence, most of my management themes are about step-change trajectory on revenues and profits.

On a lighter note, a hilarious memory from campus life is of all the teenage heartaches and heartthrobs. Who doesn't remember their 'first love'? Hours spent describing the beauty of the beloved and another few hours spent drowning the sorrows in alcohol and tears post rejection. And the same cycle (with a different muse) repeating (literally) ad nauseam over the four years. My friends and I used to organize Rose Day and man, did our club get rich. Sweet, precisely because it was so silly. But here's the thing: Each crush, successful or otherwise, who came in our lives subconsciously gifted us a clarity about the kind of person we were seeking. The few students who introspected, shifted focus from 'running behind girls' to 'finding a compatible partner.' These few, hardly half a dozen couples from our batch amidst hundreds of flings, are still going strong after twenty-five years. Ergo, clarity of thought, even in—perhaps more so in—matters of heart.

Heartbreaks in personal life and deal-breaks in the business world both provide valuable insights and clarity. They force us to reassess our priorities and desires, helping us gain a clearer vision of what we truly want. Clarity of thinking is crucial since most easy problems are generally already solved. We are not the first intelligent people looking at a challenge. Solving these difficult issues requires the hard work of peeling the onion to keep understanding the real cause. When we don't do it right, we would spend a lot of money and effort, but the wall will not move. Like Carl Jung used to say, 'All the big problems are unsolvable. But are outgrown . . . requiring a new level of consciousness,' a new level of clarity.

## Communication Skills

'Put it before them briefly so they will read it, clearly so they will appreciate it, picturesquely so they will remember it, and above all, accurately, so they will be guided by its light'—**Joseph Pulitzer, founder, Pulitzer Prize**

We all know how essential good communication is in work and life. If a leader's role is to influence, communication is the tool to make it happen. Clear, precise, impactful. Communication is less about language, and more about clarity of thought. It is much less about style and much more about substance. Over the years, I have developed a healthy distrust of people who speak pompously but hardly accurately and even less clearly.

## Think Right First, Then Communicate Right

When we are clear in our head, our communication also becomes clearer. Many people can get their point of view across to their immediate audience. This is the audience we meet everyday multiple times, so we get various opportunities to hammer the message and correct misunderstandings and clarify doubts. But as we climb the corporate ladder and communicate with a wider, multi-tiered, and geographically dispersed audience, clarity of thought—and therefore clarity of messaging—becomes essential.

At IIM Lucknow, one of the most loved courses was on Communicating to Influence. Structured along a similar course at Harvard, the first half of the course just taught us to *Think Right*, since only then can we learn to *Communicate Right*. The problem of diffused communication is often a problem of clear thinking. If we are not crystal clear in our own head, how will we make others understand it clearly? So, in a course of communication, half the classes were spent in helping students hone clear thinking. This is also why the section on communicating impactfully is part of the chapter on thinking clearly.

## Minto's Pyramid Principle

The simplest and yet most powerful concept was the Pyramid principle.[5] Barbara Minto was a consultant in McKinsey who figured out that all consultants, given their job requirement of making regular presentations to CEOs on complex problems, needed to master clear thinking. She likened good thinking to Egyptian pyramids which have withstood so many centuries of wear and tear. The structure is robust because each stone is supported by a few more stones under it. She coined the term Minto's Pyramid principle—have a clear core idea at the top and then have equally clear supporting logic to substantiate the idea. If this thinking part is done well, our communication, written or oral, is clear, concise and impactful.

## The Minto Pyramid Principle

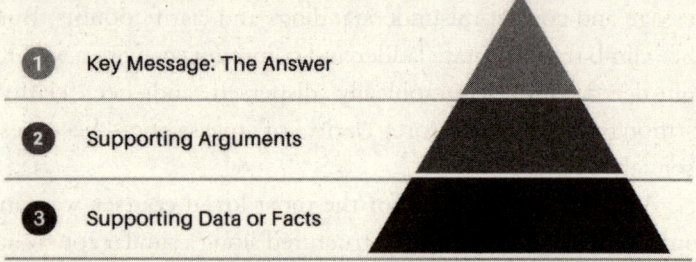

1  Key Message: The Answer

2  Supporting Arguments

3  Supporting Data or Facts

**Step 1: Define the proposal clearly in the key message**
**Step 2: Present supporting arguments**
**Step 3: Add data or fact behind each argument**

For example, imagine you are tasked with recommending an in-house music band for your company. Your Minto Pyramid might unfold as follows:

The key message: 'Our company should invest in an in-house music band run by employees.'

The supporting arguments—these could potentially be:

• It helps boost employee morale.
• It has several marketing advantages.

- It does not cost too much.

Finally, the supporting data for each argument:

- It helps boost employee morale:
  - Employee survey shows need for more fun at work.
  - Offices with more social activity show more productivity.
- It has several marketing advantages:
  - Gen Z trends suggest such things improve brand image in campus hiring.
  - Helps get free publicity of the company.

There could be other ways to structure the supporting arguments, but the concept remains the same. A clear statement supported by crisp arguments, each of which is, in turn, supported by hard data.

You will notice that since the proposal is made to the company, arguments that don't benefit the company are not part of the core recommendation. One could argue that an in-house music band could help unearth hidden talent in an employee. But a corporate effort that makes an employee a better musician will then beg the question: Why should the company invest in it? We could debate this, but the caution is to ensure your arguments are directed at what is in it for the decision maker.

## Synthesis

The other aspect of clear thinking which is very useful in communication is synthesis: The ability to see patterns and calling them out instead of just presenting raw data.

We see a colleague misplacing his wallet one day, forgetting to lock his apartment the other day and turning up late for meetings the third day. The synthesis—unspoken in itself but clear to whoever is keenly watching for patterns—is that our colleague is probably careless. Admittedly, this example may seem simplistic, but in reality, where multiple competing and overlapping symptoms exist, this synthesis requires clear thinking—the mental agility to look beyond the obvious and see not just the trees, but the entire forest.

I am flooded with emails where, as response to my query, junior team members attach a heavy Excel file with a lot of data. And assume their task is done. But what is needed is synthesis—a short summary of what the data is suggesting and how it is relevant to the query being asked. In my growing up years, a lot of my reputation in P&G came from nicely drafted email with insights from data analysis and a clear recommendation and action step.

## Precision

And we learnt precise writing. The art of putting maximum content in minimum words. Not an iota of verbiage. Like the famous author of *Le Petit Prince*, Antoine de Saint-Exupéry claimed: 'Perfection is achieved, not when there is nothing more to add, but when there is nothing left to take away.' There is this famous anecdote where a leader was asked when he was available to deliver a speech. His curt reply, 'If you want me to speak for 10 min, I need a week to prepare. If you want me to speak for an hour, I am ready now.'[6]

In my early corporate years, my boss coached me to spend about half an hour meditating before every important meeting—reflecting on key points, clarifying my thoughts, and ensuring I was clear on what I needed others to understand just as well as I did.

Always start with an elevator speech. In other words, if we were riding an elevator with the CEO and he asked us what we were going to present today, how would we answer him in just a few sentences? In the limited time we have till the elevator reaches the floor. This clarity helps if our presentation time gets shortened at the last minute. Don't try to cram thirty minutes of content into a ten-minute time slot. Cut out the background and articulate just the elevator pitch. Clarity of thought is essential in achieving this—unless we are clear in our own head what the core message is, how will we create an elevator pitch. Hence thinking right precedes communicating right.

So, leaders who want to influence others must learn to communicate well. Which, in turn, first requires learning to think clearly. Everyday, in good and bad months, I have to articulate an inspiring vision of how we will become better, with an equally compelling supporting logic.

## Clarity in Personal Career Management

We just saw that clearer the message, the greater its impact. Likewise, possessing clarity of thought about our career can help us have a successful and fulfilling career.

A consulting friend showed me statistics on India's kabbadi players vs cricket players. Very similar effort and input, but such a vast difference in fame and money. He dryly quipped that more important than how well you do is where you stand.

So then, how do we get clarity on where to stand? Many young students ask me what their career choice should be. The model I recommended to my own kids is the Japanese Ikigai[7], finding the passion that gives value and joy to life. To identify this passion, look at the Venn Diagram[8] below with the four categories of 'what we love,' 'what the world needs,' 'what we can be paid for,' and 'what we are good at.'

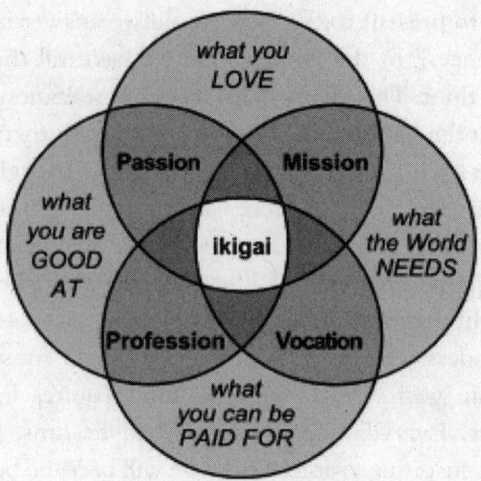

Our ideal pursuit—that will give both value *and* joy—needs to be at the confluence of all these four. Often, we choose a corporate job that the world needs and which can pay us, but we don't really love the work. Then it will be difficult to excel in it since a part of us is not passionate about it and will perhaps burn out. On the other hand, there could be hobbies like music or acting which we loved in school, but we may realize that getting paid for it could be difficult given the heavy competition.

Our life's true Ikigai needs all four. Like Elon Musk's pursuit of electric cars—he loves these innovations, the world desperately needs to move out of carbon fuels, consumers are willing to pay a premium for noiseless smokeless Teslas, and Musk is personally brilliant in the engineering skills developing such a car requires. I was reading about the founders of the dozen or so unicorns (billion dollar valued start-ups) India has created in recent years. Many of them found their Ikigai in their venture.

A sobering thought: Till we find something that can cover all four circles, my suggestion will be to find what covers most circles and have outside hobbies to cover the remaining.

When our batch joined P&G fresh out of campus, a senior leader asked us what we wanted in life. What should a job give so that we will call it a great choice. All of twenty years of age, most of us put the usual adjectives on the white board: money, name, power, social impact, work-life balance. He then asked us which profession will give us all of these. Unfortunately, not a single option emerged. We could join, say, civil services for power, but at least in those days, it did not pay as much as an MNC. We could join an NGO for social impact but again money may not follow. On the other hand, in a typical entry level corporate job, the money may be okay, but real social impact was often questionable. So, his advice was, find a job that gives you most of the attributes you want, and then, alongside that, choose a healthy hobby or weekend passion that fulfils the other yearnings. This simple clarity allowed us to live fully, rather than dwell on what we lacked.

## Footprints in the Sand: Our purpose in life

'And now with old age,
It's become very clear,
Things I once found important,
Were not why I was here'
　　　　—*The True Meaning Of Life* by Pat A. Fleming

At some age, we move from personal career preference to a personal vision—what do we want to be remembered for. What legacy do we want to leave? Our footprints in the sand. The meaning in our life.

Viktor Frankl's theory, Logotherapy (Greek: logos— meaning), says that we are happy when we find a meaning, a contribution and a calling in life. Life without purpose, even with all comfort, will be hollow and aimless.[9] On the contrary, a life of meaning will keep us going, even in the harshest of circumstances. This philosophy is very different from other psychologists like Freud, who believed that life was largely a 'pursuit for pleasure' or Alder, who spoke of life as a constant 'desire for power.' Dr Frankl illustrates that when the will to find meaning in life is lost—when we fall into an existential vacuum, unsure of our purpose—we are left in despair. Even our physical immunity reduces, leading to various ailments.

This *pursuit of meaning* might surface in our work, driving us to do something personally fulfilling, or in love, where we're moved to deeply care for another. It could just be the resolve to come out of a difficult situation unscathed. Man's search for this purpose and meaning can be a very powerful driver leading to self-transcendence. In this pursuit of meaning, clarity of thought guides us through the fog of uncertainty. It is the skill of clear thinking that will illuminate one's purpose.

The 'meaning of life' can be different for different people and even different at different times. There is an interesting anecdote that Peter Druker, the father of management, wrote in his memoirs.[10] His father and he went to meet the famous economist Joseph Schumpeter, an old friend of his father's:

> Suddenly, my father asked with a chuckle, 'Joseph, do you still talk about what you want to be remembered for?' Schumpeter broke out in loud laughter.

For Schumpeter was notorious for having said, when he was 30 or so and had published the first two of his great economics books, that what he really wanted to be remembered for was having been 'Europe's greatest lover of beautiful women and Europe's greatest horseman—and perhaps also the world's greatest economist.'

Schumpeter said, 'Yes, this question is still important to me, but I now answer it differently. I want to be remembered as having been the teacher who converted half a dozen brilliant students into first-rate economists.'

He must have seen an amazed look on my father's face, because he continued, 'You know, Adolph, I have now reached the age where I know that being remembered for books and theories is not enough. One does not make a difference unless it is a difference in the lives of people.'

One reason my father had gone to see Schumpeter was that it was known that the economist was very sick and would not live long. Schumpeter died five days after we visited him.

I learned from it three things: First, one has to ask oneself what one wants to be remembered for. Second, that should change. It should change both with one's own maturity and with changes in the world. Finally, one thing worth being remembered for is the difference one makes in the lives of people.

About Elon Musk, his HR head said: 'He so clearly sees his vision unfolding that it is unfathomable that it won't happen.' He regularly puts most of his own money (from previous start-ups) in his new idea. This level of conviction can only happen once we see things clearly in our head. So, finding our true calling, our vision for life, is less about age, and more about maturity and clarity.

We have heard in various places that when we genuinely want something, the universe conspires to help us achieve it. I suspect, minus the mystical, it alludes to first having clear thinking on what we want, and then having the passion to pursue it. After all, in Shah Rukh Khan's words (in the movie *Om Shanti Om*) that resonate with the hopeful dreamer in all of us, '*Kehte hain agar kisi cheez ko dil se chaho, to poori kainaat use tumse milane ki koshish mein lag jaati hai*' [The universe conspires to help you if you passionately want something]. And in that chase, every *Om* finds his *Shanti*, every dreamer their destiny, not merely by wishing upon a star but by nurturing a vision with the kind of clarity that makes the seemingly impossible, inevitable.

## Summary

- Clear thinking is essential in problem-solving, especially in complex situations where multiple symptoms may cloud judgment.

- Identifying the root cause, the one or two prime drivers, amidst various symptoms, is crucial for effective problem-solving.

- Failure to address the core issue leads to wasted resources and persistent problems.

- Even otherwise intelligent individuals often respond from biases, focusing on associated symptoms rather than the main issue, leading to wrong decision making.

- The scientific method of questioning and probing separates incorrect hypotheses from the real problem.

- Be clear of Right to Win, what is unique about us that will allow us to win amidst competition.

- Contextual Familiarity: Understand how the world actually works. This will require going beyond armchair theory and desktop research.

- Clear thinking leads to clear communication, and hence our ability to influence others.
    - Minto's Pyramid principle encourages us to have a clear governing statement with supporting logic.
    - Synthesis: Present insights and not raw data, by identifying patterns.
    - Precision: Maximum content, minimum verbosity.

- Clear thinking is also crucial in personal career management, using Ikigai to find fulfilment in both personal as well as professional pursuits. Ikigai links one's passion and strengths with what the world needs and is willing to pay for.
- In reality, our career may not provide all we seek. Find the closest match and then develop active interests outside work.
- At some age, at some level of maturity and clarity, we move from career to life's calling. The will to meaning. This may change with the stage of our life.

## Food for Thought: Self-Assessment

1.  In problem-solving, have I consistently taken the time to uncover the underlying causes behind superficial symptoms? Is there a tendency to rely on quick fixes without fully understanding the root cause of the problem?

2.  Consider a real-life problem at work that is not being resolved. What associated issues and distractions are preventing clear identification of the root cause? What biases of the players involved might be further clouding the issue? How would I peel the onion?

3.  Reflect on a real-life corporate decision. Did I observe preconceived biases or flawed thinking that led to errors in judgment? This might include being misled by past successes, confusing cause with effect, or continuing with a fundamentally broken initiative due to emotional attachment. How could such errors be avoided in the future? What about my personal experiences—were there instances where erroneous decisions were made?

4.  When was the last time I was asked to provide views on a topic without having direct, on-the-ground knowledge of how things really worked? What steps can be taken to quickly develop contextual familiarity in such situations?

5. Reflecting on past experiences of addressing a group, did I find that influencing others was more effective when I was thoroughly prepared and clear-headed compared to speaking spontaneously?

6. What is my Ikigai—the passion that provides both value and joy? How can the four concentric circles of Ikigai be filled with possibilities to ultimately identify what lies at their intersection? Over time, can I articulate a life purpose that I want to be remembered for?

# 5

## Focus

'Time is flying, never to return'—**Virgil, regarded as ancient Rome's greatest poet**

'Stop adding, start deleting! Winning demands total focus'—**Michael Jordan, basketball legend, first billionaire player in NBA history**

When I became CEO, time and energy suddenly became my most precious resources. It was the same me, and the day had the same twenty-four hours, but the responsibilities and complexities had increased manifold. I was already working hard, and the path of 'working even harder as responsibilities became even bigger' did not appeal to me. Beyond the impossibility of continuing to work harder every time, it would also lead to a broken family and a burnt-out self. After all, work literally expands to fill all the time available.

Instead, the magic word is FOCUS.

I often hear people compliment how I manage to accomplish much within the same twenty-four hours. Besides being a full-time CEO, I also chair the board's Nomination

& Remuneration committee at a leading business school, write books, run a thriving book blog and invest in multiple companies.

I have tried not to have my life usurped by just work. At home, I stay actively involved: teaching my kids, sharing daily tea with my wife, catching up with my parents every day and never missing out on vacations.

I also carve out time for my passions. I have explored eighty countries (business trips don't count), took on adrenaline-fuelled adventures (flying small planes, snake handling, bungee jumping and skydiving) and taught at universities. I unwind by binging on Netflix on the couch just like any other person (*Lucifer* and *Bandish Bandits* are absolute favourites).

This chapter enumerates the top six tips that have worked for me. But before we begin, let's introduce the readers to some quintessential time management personas we see every day around us:

- **The Fireman:** Everything feels like a 'crisis' for the fireman. Time management becomes extinguishing one blazing deadline after another.
- **The Yes Man:** With a heart bigger than their calendar, they have a penchant for saying 'yes' to everything (usually to their own detriment).
- **The Procrastinator:** The master of 'later,' their time management involves a lot of postponing until the pressure mounts to a point where action becomes unavoidable.

As the chapter progresses, readers may find themselves resonating with one or more of these personalities at different times.

## 1. Manage Priorities, not Time

Efficiency is trying to do more in less time while effectiveness is focusing on the right things. The starting point is not the calendar and a mad race to fit everything in it. Instead, the starting point is identifying the few key things that, if done well, will lead to great results. The few projects that can step-change business or life trajectory must take the lion's share of our time. Big impact on the big things.

In my role spanning eighty different countries, everything cries for attention. In the beginning, each opportunity and minor crisis kept me busy whole day long. But I soon realized that even when we were executing those well, they were hardly creating a meaningful impact on overall business. There were small markets which, even if we did everything right, would grow an extra million, miniscule in consolidation, but consuming the same effort as other projects that could generate 10x value. Small deals took similar time, effort and energy as large deals, but their impact was negligible. Over time, I started rationalizing my time to mainly get involved in things that had high impact potential. In retrospect, this may seem like common sense, but I can vouch that when every idea looks promising and every young manager eagerly seeks the CEO's attention, it's easy to get caught up in the thick of thin things—working hard day and night but still not making progress in what matters most.

Many people rush through their days in a frenzy of activity but achieve little because they fail to focus on what truly matters. At the heart of time management is an important shift in focus: Select few key priorities, instead of trying to fit everything in.

I also realized one email from me created a chain of twenty emails down the hierarchy. Whatever the CEO focusses on generally does well, but, in a zero-sum game of organizational resources and priority, the non-focus areas tend to go downhill. The race is then whether the enterprise nets off to growth or decline.

In our annual performance appraisal, I started to look at how much time in the year the team spent on the things that created the maximum impact in our business performance. The answer is rarely more than 20 per cent. What happened to the remaining 80 per cent effort? Sadly, 80 per cent of all our effort is wasted,[1] in the sense that it achieves too little impact weighed against the effort.

Our final performance record, even our resume, is supposed to be a list of achievements, not a list of activities. So, focus on big results in a few things, and not on the width of activities. In the famous HBR paper *Beware the Busy Manager*, the authors lament that: (With most managers) 'you'll see an astonishing amount of fast-moving activity that allows almost no time for reflection.' They coin a term 'unproductive busyness.' Their finding is that 90 per cent of managers squander their time in all sorts of ineffective activities. Only '10 per cent of managers spend their time in a committed, purposeful and reflective manner.'[2] To be clear, the former are not lazy people. On the contrary, they are one of our hardest working people. Unfortunately, they keep pushing the wall which does not move.

Case in point: A colleague asks the Yes Man to review a report due tomorrow—he agrees. His boss assigns him a last-minute presentation—he agrees with no hesitation. Meanwhile, his team needs his input on a critical project, and he does not want to disappoint them either, so he commits to joining their brainstorming session. While this eagerness may seem admirable to us, it often leaves the Yes Man overburdened, and unable to focus on what truly matters.

The same happens in relationships. Think of the best moments with our special someone. What per cent of time together were these memorable moments? Generally, a small fraction. Where did the remaining go?

Prioritization first requires being crystal clear on the roles we are playing. (Which is also why the chapter on clarity of thought must precede the chapter on focus.) One person can play maybe five to seven roles well at any point in time. In my case, I am a CEO, an author, an investor, a husband, a father, a son and a friend. Define these clearly and identify the big priorities in each. If the roles are increasing, be prepared to give up something.

One of my friends was a vice president at P&G. He used to play golf on the weekends. But when he became a father, he happily dropped this habit by saying he had to give up an existing role to meaningfully take on a new role. Weekdays were frenetic for him anyway, and if weekends were also booked for golf, he reckoned he wouldn't be able to fulfil his parental responsibility of devoting time to his child.

People (procrastinators, I am looking at you) tend to neglect priority setting because it requires deep thinking. What they fail to consider is that a little time and effort put in early saves an enormous amount of time, effort and frustration in the future. I suspect the real reason we put off priority setting is because it requires clear thinking and clarity on what exactly are the big rocks in our life. Often, we have only a faint idea of what truly matters, as gaining clarity requires quiet time and deep reflection. This 'me time' is not default for most people, since we are most used to a life of claustrophobic chaos with every minute of our life packed with stimuli. But unless we choose our own priorities, life and those around us end up choosing for us. Casual friends may drop in and we end up spending an hour entertaining them with wine, food and conversations. Nothing wrong in that per se; all work and no play does make Jack a dull boy. But beware if it is coming at the cost of neglecting something which was more important in our life's mission.

Ask: Who is controlling our life? It should not be on autopilot, letting others dictate our priorities.

## 2. Manage Distractions

In P&G, our then India CEO, Shantanu Khosla (later, managing director of Crompton Greaves), was famed to have a clean desk. No one ever saw any file or papers on his table. He would review, give his inputs, ensure a team was there to take notes and then move to another meeting. He used to say, a clean desk is a symbol of a clean mind.

And yet, for most of us, daily operations cry for attention, tempting our involvement. Only to suck us up, working hard but not reaching anywhere. The distraction is not just a time robber, it is also an energy drainer and mind clutterer. The yes men get into this trap all the time. I used to be very proud of replying to all my emails within few hours but have now started wondering if it—fast replies even on small things—is worth it in the first place.

The average employee gets interrupted fifty to sixty times per day, with nearly 80 per cent of these interruptions being unimportant. As a result, most people spend little time in what psychologists call the 'flow state'—a space where productivity can be up to five times higher.[3]

The best of us take the concept of avoiding distractions to the next level. Mark Zuckerberg wears t-shirts of the same colour every day to office. His logic is that these little distractions (like choosing new clothing every day) over time take a lot of unnecessary mind space, hence life must be simplified. There's a famous anecdote, often attributed to Einstein, in which he looked up his own phone number in the directory when asked for it. People asked him how he couldn't recall his own phone number, and his retort was, 'Why memorize something that I can look up.'

In Sir Arthur Conan Doyle's books, the iconic deerstalker hat-wearing detective, Sherlock Holmes, does not know the Earth revolves around the Sun—and for good reason. To him, such rudimentary details about the solar system were irrelevant. He did, however, know London's labyrinth of streets very well. Holmes likened his brain to an attic: Space is limited, so it must be used wisely.

Mind decluttering is very important. We may not be physically working on a project but mentally we still keep thinking about it. Just before bed, my mind is often a whirlwind of thoughts, making it hard to sleep. The practice of writing things down helps. I now have a post-it and pen on my bed side table, where I jot down whatever is in my mind. It sends a signal to the brain that this is taken care of, and the brain can stop worrying.

I get about 150 emails a day. I try to categorize them into:

- Critical for our business priorities: Only 20 per cent of emails are usually linked to critical priorities, needing my direct involvement.
- Not critical but important enough for me to monitor personally: This category needs effective delegation, and I only monitor, not act.
- Not meaningful enough for my personal involvement: This requires telling the senders to stop copying me, and in some cases, killing off those projects all together.

One more trick that helps declutter the mind is to refer to a document/ email only once (either respond or delete, but don't come back to it).

That and yes, I have switched off all push notifications on my phone. I literally counted that between Uber and banking and WhatsApp and email, I was getting forty to fifty notifications a day. A hyperconnected stage does not allow us to reflect, recharge and focus. Some experts recommend set time slots—say six times a day—to look at emails or messages, though I haven't been able to discipline myself that much. The month I became CEO, I politely exited from all family and school/ college WhatsApp groups. Just checking the latest comment by someone was an avoidable distraction.

Of course, the biggest distractions are office meetings. About half our time goes in meetings. My own take is that most have too many participants, are too long, do not have a clear agenda and are generally boring. Hence, smart people have found their hacks. Richard Branson pushes for standing meetings with no chairs; Jeff Bezos has banned Powerpoint presentations in meetings; Facebook limits participants to six to eight.

Strategy is also a choice of what not to do. It is OKAY to say NO to requests (again, the yes man's dilemma), to decline additional responsibilities, to ask for additional resources/ time. Quality execution of the task in hand always trumps multiple tasks shabbily done at once. Don't bite off more than you can chew.

Neuroscience now tells us that our brain does not really multi task, but switches tasks—on and off—very quickly. So multi tasking is fine for mundane, low-end tasks like listening to music on the car speaker while driving in a familiar territory. But it is not advisable when doing deep work, which requires serious thinking. In fact, multi tasking while doing deep thinking causes stress and reduces effectiveness.[4]

In the busiest of times, slow down and get some time to stand and stare. Warren Buffett, ever the polite, humble and friendly man, still regularly says 'No' to the vast majority of people who attempt to divert his attention. When a famous journalist asked to interview him about his hero, Benjamin Graham, Buffett declined, saying: 'Thanks for the invitation, but I'll have to decline. I've talked about Ben on a number of occasions, so my appraisal of him is already out there for people to see. In addition, every interview I grant results in about twenty more requests. That's a geometric progression that I have no inclination to foster.'[5]

This discipline is even more important in personal activities. Every day, a whirlwind of tasks vies for my attention the moment I step into my house. There might be a pipe under the sink mocking me with its persistent drip, a friend or family member eyeing me as their personal Uber for shopping errands and, of course, there is the tedious task of booking personal travel tickets. The advice I follow is to set and enforce an aspirational personal hourly rate. Hopefully at least as much as our current hourly salary, but ideally even more. If fixing a problem will save less than your hourly rate, ignore it. If outsourcing a task will cost less than your hourly rate, outsource it.[6]

This is not about attaching our worth to a number but about recognizing the finite nature of our time. Even as trite as the 'Time is money' saying goes, its relevance never fades. Think about the way the English language treats time—we 'spend' or 'save' time like we do money. And yet, 'we think much more about the use of money, which is renewable, than we do about the use of our time, which is irreplaceable.'[7]

## 3. Delegate Effectively

Before starting to work on a task, ask whether you are the most appropriate person to complete it. Are there people below who, with some coaching, can take over this task in the future? This is not just true for work, but also for personal life. Is there a younger sibling or a house help who, with some handholding, can start owning a regular piece of work and free up your time?

In fact, why restrict it to people below?

Delegation can be done at all levels—downward, horizontal and upward. Sometimes our managers, because of their larger remit or experience or authority, can close in one hour what would take us a day. Why not delegate to them?

The gold standard is perhaps Warren Buffett who has designed his life such that his own schedule is blissfully uncluttered, leaving him to spend much of his time reading and thinking without distractions. His daily to-do list, chairing a multi hundred billion enterprise, is barely a few items in a small diary.

While everyone agrees on the need for delegation, few people are effective in it. There are always:

The Over Delegators: People who assume the team will do everything. Since they are not on top of what is happening, they are utlimately unable to help immediately when things get stuck. They act as a postbox without much value add. They would make general statements on motivation of their team, but very soon their own manager starts talking directly to their team.

The Under Delegators: People who have not moved on from their previous one level below role. Since they were good at doing it, they want to continue doing it. Even if they give the task to someone else, they micromanage, taking all ownership away from others.

Good delegators maintain a balance, delegating but not abdicating. They sit with the team early on, share specific expectations, ask for clarifications and upfront clear the rules of the game (deadline, quality, resources). They then monitor progress regularly and make themselves available for support. They delegate the task but not the accountability.

## 4. Manage Energy, not Time

Our fast-paced life has many energy drainers: stressful meetings, deadlines, business risks, difficult relationships at office and at home, guilt over not giving enough time to loved ones, responsibilities at home which call in the evening just when you want to take rest from office work, health issues that may keep popping up from time to time, insecurities—both financial and emotional. The list is endless.

Arguments—at office or at home—are the worst. It is rarely about the physical time spent on them, but the emotional toll they take, sapping our energy as we keep thinking about them. Our mind keeps constructing alternate scenarios and keeps debating with the other person who is not even there. This can be terribly frustrating. A discussion is supposed to be a clash of ideas, so that the best one wins and together we choose better alternatives than what one person could think of. Sadly, it usually becomes a clash of egos, making us lose time and peace of mind without any productive gain.

In the corporate world, at least in some less evolved companies, there exists an unspoken agreement between organizations and their employees[8]—a tacit pact, if you will. Each party strives to extract as much as they can from the other (as efficiently as they can), only to eventually part ways without a backward glance. However, this only results in mutual exhaustion and dissatisfaction. Hence, the need to consciously manage our energy levels.

The most common energy robber is anger or frustration. Buddhists equate anger with holding a burning coal in our hands while waiting to throw it at others. Holding onto the coal is not only futile, but also inflicts self-pain. That's why one of my favourite quotes is: 'Forgive others, not because they deserve forgiveness but because you deserve peace.'

One of my former bosses habitually took a walk after every difficult meeting. Walking helps not just to clear the muck but also to gain perspective. Another good CEO friend, after a stressful day at office, goes for a jog and keeps running till he can run no more. The strenuous run melts his stress away as he is too physically exhausted to think of anything. I have seen him walk back relaxed and smiling. Another friend, CEO of a headhunting firm, has this retort ready every time his wife and he (both good singers) are about to get into a tiff: 'Let's not fight, let's sing instead!'

The dietary aspect of energy boosters is just as crucial. Eating right—less carbs, less sugar, less oil—staying healthy with a daily protein shake and salads for lunch, and practising moderation (one coffee or tea a day, at least two liters of water) are timeless tips. So is staying active. I always feel more energetic and relaxed on days I hit the gym, swim, or even manage some light yoga and meditation.

## 5. Living a Quadrant II Life

'I have two kinds of problems: the urgent and the important. The urgent are not important, and the important are never urgent'—**Dwight Eisenhower, former US president, in a 1954 speech**

Covey popularized the Time Management Matrix[9] that divided all our tasks into either urgent or important (image below). The quadrant where people spend most time is urgent and important—think about deadlines, angry bosses, demanding clients, etc. These are typically 'fires' that need to be put out immediately, both urgent as also alarmingly important. These suit our fireman personality type.

The trouble with leading a life largely in this quadrant is that the organization does not improve. Next week, there will be another fire on some other topic, and so on till the point where employees burn out. How do we think of thriving—achieving long term strategy or aspirational goals—when much of our time is consumed in mere existing?

Covey strongly recommended living in Quadrant II, which was about activities deemed not urgent but still important. Think planning, training, relationship building, analysis, brainstorming—all crucial for long term success but with no external deadline looming over them. While we may be intellectually convinced of their importance, in practice, we hardly spend proactive time here. My own assessment is that people spend 20 per cent time here when they should be spending 50 per cent. The thing which most people (especially the fireman personality type) miss out on is: if we do Quadrant II well, it will automatically avoid fires in future.

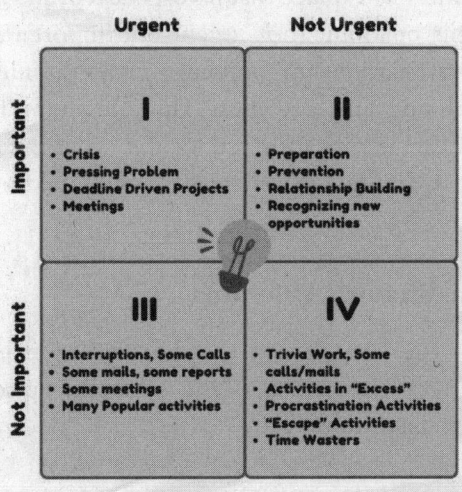

There is this interview about a top performing city firefighting department. Literally the name itself suggests handling fires, and one would think the top performers would have a very efficient model to quickly douse wherever and whenever a fire broke out. But their chief explained what made them the best: They analysed past data on what generally caused most fires and spent a lot of time in inspecting buildings and generating awareness amongst citizens around these causes. This—analysis, prevention and relationship building—ensures the incidence of fires itself reduces in the first place, making them the best performing fire department. Risk assessment and prevention, community outreach, training and education—boring as they may sound—deliver much better output than efficiency and crises management. The key to breaking free from the cycle of crises management lies not in perfecting the science of firefighting but in mastering the art of fire prevention.

Think about the equivalent of it at corporate. Instead of an endless cycle of quenching metaphorical fires—rushing to meet unexpected deadlines, addressing client crises at the eleventh hour—imagine a workplace that invests heavily in Quadrant II activities. This quadrant (not urgent but important) includes tasks such as relationship building, market understanding, employee training and analytics. This Quadrant II focused organization can significantly reduce the occurrence of crises by switching from being perpetually reactive to thoughtfully proactive.

## The Procrastinator's Dilemma

'I'll get to it later' has led to the downfall of many a good employee. After too many 'laters' the work piles up so high that any task seems insurmountable.

AA was a participant in our *Timeless Skills* workshop and shared his learnings on why he tended to delay tasks. A common cause was feeling overwhelmed by the task. Often these were Quadrant II activities, for example, brainstorming growth opportunities in his region South-east Asia. There was an element of vagueness, and one did not really know where to begin. There was limited external pressure to complete the task immediately. He also doubted whether his team had the skills or resources needed to complete such an analysis on this relatively new region. So, he found solace in tackling the immediate tasks he knew he could complete with ease. He still was busy, but by spending extra time on mundane stuff and putting off strategic Quadrant II stuff. Over time, he realized that the big tasks weren't going away—truly important tasks rarely do. Worse, he could be seen by management as indecisive, slow and not strategic enough as the step-change tasks were getting de-prioritized. With this new awareness built in the workshop, and his own introspection, he was able to make a conscious effort. Using tools like blocking calendar in advance for his self-driven priorities, he was able to start and complete some big projects.

## Attack Root Causes

There was an ambitious and hard-working chartered accountant in our team who was always putting in overtime. Working with a poor work-life balance for a long time, he ultimately started showing signs of a burnout. His manager suggested we hire more people to share his workload. I requested for a deep dive: why exactly was there so much overwork?

The findings showed us that overtime was just a symptom. The real problems were:

1. **Poor automation:** System reports were taking too long, and were not in the format requested by management, so they required manual intervention.

2. **Poor knowledge:** The person did not know the advance features of enterprise system, and even of Microsoft Excel. Hence, he took more time to do things.

3. **Poor collaboration:** Cross functional stakeholders did not respond in time or were working in silos. Half his overtime was due to lack of timely support.

4. **Poor processes:** The workflow was broken causing significant rework. Someone would post a 'surprise entry' requiring him to redo month end closing.

5. **Unrealistic expectations:** Too much stress in role requiring him to deliver +/ -1 per cent accuracy of forecast when the fundamental drivers of forecasting were broken.

Unless we fixed this, adding more people in that department wouldn't solve the fundamental problem. Lack of time is usually only a symptom. The root cause is usually failure in some Quadrant II activity and the above five—automation, training, relationship building, process improvements and stakeholder management—will thus keep coming back to haunt us.

## 6. Calendar Management

Every Friday, I sit with my secretary and identify my 'big rocks' for the coming week, the few things that will make a big difference. Then my secretary blocks these on my calendar. Some of these could be meetings with myself or even some quiet time focused on a specific area.

Covey used to say, 'Things that matter most must never be at the mercy of things that matter less.' And yet, in the rigmarole and chaos of daily work, we let priority B, C and D keep us busy and away from priority A. Because the daily fires are immediate, urgent and ever present, constantly demanding our time and filling our schedules with back-to-back meetings. On the other hand, the biggest priorities often necessitate time with ourselves: quiet reflection, deep analysis, building relationships, making cold calls, etc. None of these are urgent, none of the managers are 'ordering' us to complete these and so they keep getting pushed back. Hence, I block the time needed to complete these Quadrant II activities myself formally in the calendar.

This means that sometimes my secretary has to decline other meetings since there is no place left in the calendar. That is fine. Stay focused—key things must happen superbly, even if others fall off the plate. Otherwise, work will expand to fill in the entire time available. In fact, as I became senior, I started blocking off entire Fridays just for Quadrant II activities— strategy discussions, people reviews, customer connects. Nothing operational, no firefighting on Fridays, only longer-term impact projects. (Bill Gates is famous for his annual 'Think Week' ritual, where he goes off the grid to think for an entire week.)

To operationally help with calendar blocking, one should ask:

- What are our key roles?
- What is our ultimate goal in those roles?
- What is the most important thing we can do in each role within this planning bucket (i.e., the coming week)?

And then . . .

- Put down and block time for those activities (that help meet the key goals) formally in calendar (commit to them)
- Allocate only the remaining time for 'regular activities'
- Follow with discipline

For example, one of the key roles in my own life is being a husband. My ultimate goal is to be a loving, caring and understanding husband. Each of these adjectives requires very different behaviour—one can be very loving but not understanding. These three are things I know my wife craves and I would love for her to use these three adjectives, perhaps in my epitaph, when she is finally describing me. Each would then require specific activities. For example, for loving, I schedule a date with her every month in a nice restaurant (yes, even after twenty-five years). For caring, I talk to her parents every weekend and also schedule a time once a month where she talks of all her problems and I just try to listen ('try to' . . . this one is never easy, men are programmed to start giving logical solutions instead of just hearing). Understanding is still work in progress.

One learning is not to over schedule. Allow some flexible time (say 30 per cent) for crisis and unforeseen priorities that will invariably come uninvited and ask for time. And keep buffers, at least fifteen minutes of free time (ideally thirty) between two meetings. Back-to-back meetings, the norm in corporate, make us chase our tail the entire day as one meeting spills over, leaving little time to consolidate our thinking.

By the way, to each his own. I read somewhere that Bill Gates manages his calendar with total precision: It features maniacally detailed entries such as '6:47 shower' and '6:57 shave.'

## Case Study:

(Based on a real-life incident narrated by a colleague of mine. Names have been changed.)

Sameer was a marketing MBA and got a campus placement in a leading bank, beating thirty other students who appeared for that vacancy for the post of area sales manager. He was reporting to regional sales head, SK.

Sameer not only performed well in the induction programme but also did reasonably well initially in delivering his sales targets. During this period, the bank was in aggressive expansion mode and branch output was watched with hawk eyes by top management. In no time, Sameer realized that sales was no mean task, and he started feeling the heat. The pressure kept on building on all the branches of the bank.

Sameer was quite social by nature. He frequently got involved in attending marriages, parties and all sorts of batch get-togethers. He had a close friend PK who used to commute with Sameer in Sameer's vehicle. PK, in the accounts department, had to stay late in the office. Sameer would wait for him and then they both used to leave office quite late. To unwind in the evening, Sameer used to chat on the net. His job was becoming more and more high pressure, and so to relax, by and by Sameer got addicted to chatting.

As sometimes happens in sales, one quarter did not go well for Sameer. He received a 'pep talk' from his national head for that. Owing to his addiction, coupled with a desire to vent off his tension, Sameer started chatting in the office on his system.

His normal routine would be:

> Come to office, make couple of sales calls in the field, come back to office and chat for couple of hours, meet with his boss, wait for PK, and while waiting, chat again.
>
> His sales figures went downhill, and his boss SK was under pressure to take a call on Sameer's future in the bank. One day, his boss caught him chatting. Without hesitation, he was summoned to the cabin and given a choice—resign within a month or face termination.
>
> Looking back, it's clear that Sameer was slipping deeper into a rabbit hole. But while he was actually there, every incremental activity—an extra friends' party, a little chat, a little wait for PK, one quarter of poor performance—did not appear individually alarming. And yet, they all added up and resulted in his firing.

What seem like small, seemingly innocuous habits snowball into significant issues over time.

## Reflection Tool: Time Management Log

I ask all my teams to track their daily schedule for a fortnight. For any two 'regular' weeks, plot every single activity during working hours and then group them into broad themes and calculate the percentage of time spent in each.

When I last did it for myself as CEO, most of my time was going in the following buckets: business reviews, quarterly target chasing, strategic projects, people connect, hunting/customer connect calls, etc. The themes were fine, but the data showed I was spending too much time on operations/ supply management (target 5 per cent of time, actual 10 per cent) and too little time on new launches (target 10 per cent, actual 4 per cent). This would hijack the growth agenda of the business.

The biggest disappointment was something else. Almost 25–30 per cent of my time was unaccounted for! I knew I was in office for that time and busy, but I could not identify any purposeful work I did. Time management gurus warn us—you add up all the things you consciously did in a day and that will always come to twenty to twenty-one hours instead of twenty four hours. Little distractions, interruptions and other wastages that we don't realize at that moment, all add up. Pragmatically, this will never be zero, but maybe we can bring it down to 10 per cent? That will save us one to two hours every single day.

Do this yourself (see annexure on my own sample time log) to ensure your time tomorrow is better spent than your time today.

Also take the Time Management Assessment (annexure) to see where exactly your improvement area is. After all, Einstein couldn't have been more right when he claimed, 'Insanity is doing the same thing again and again expecting a different result.'

# Annexure 1: Fortnightly Time Management Log, Nishant Saxena

(edited to remove company specific events)

Total Work Hours: 100 hours (10 hours a day * 5 days per week * 2 weeks)

| S. No | Themes | Work Description | Hrs | Actual % | Proposed % |
|---|---|---|---|---|---|
| 1 | P&L Monitoring | Month—current | 1 | | |
| | | Month—next | 1 | 4 | 5 |
| | | Quarter—current | 1 | | |
| | | Orderbook—next month | 1 | | |
| 2 | Business Review | Direct markets | 2 | | |
| | | Indirect markets | 2 | 8 | 10 |
| | | Profit plan/ COGS | 2 | | |
| | | Marketing | 2 | | |
| 3 | Strategy Projects | 5-year plans | 1 | | |
| | | Localizations | 1 | 4 | 5 |
| | | Country model change | 2 | | |
| 4 | Supply Chain | Weekly reviews | 2 | | |
| | | Product issues | 2 | 10 | 5 |
| | | Third party sources | 6 | | |

| S. No | Themes | Work Description | Hrs | Actual % | Proposed % |
|---|---|---|---|---|---|
| 5 | HR | Increments/ Ratings | 2 | 4 | 5 |
| | | Culture building projects | 2 | | |
| 6 | R&D | New products | 1 | | 10 |
| | | New markets | 2 | 4 | |
| | | Product improvements | 1 | | |
| 7 | Board Meetings | As chair | 1 | | 5 |
| | | As member | 1 | 4 | |
| | | As observer | 2 | | |
| 8 | Personal | Self coaching | 1 | | 2 |
| | | Reading | 1 | 2 | |
| 9 | Approvals | Various proposals | 4 | 4 | 5 |
| 10 | People Connect | N-1 | 1 | | 5 |
| | | N-2 | 1 | 6 | |
| | | Juniors | 2 | | |
| | | New hires | 2 | | |

| S. No | Themes | Work Description | Hrs | Actual % | Proposed % |
|---|---|---|---|---|---|
| 11 | Growth/Hunting | Unsolicited reachouts | 2 | | |
| | | Existing partner connects | 2 | | |
| | | Focus market growth | 2 | | |
| | | New processes | 2 | | |
| | | Data analytics/ Opportunities | 2 | 18 | 20 |
| | | Business Development/ Inorganic brainstorming | 2 | | |
| | | General Exports opps | 2 | | |
| | | Next fiscal Projections | 4 | | |
| 12 | Efficiencies | Dashboards | 2 | | |
| | | Losses | 2 | 4 | 3 |
| 13 | Others/unaccounted | Many small little things | 28 | 28 | 20 |
| | | | 100 | 100 | 100 |

# Annexure 2: Time Management Self-Assessment

For each question, honestly rate yourself: Always, Never, Sometimes

| | |
|---|---|
| 1 | Are the tasks you work on during the day the ones with the highest priority? |
| 2 | Do you find yourself completing tasks at the last minute or asking for extensions? |
| 3 | Do you set aside time for planning and scheduling? |
| 4 | Do you know how much time you are spending on the various jobs you do? |
| 5 | Do you often find various interruptions when doing important things? |
| 6 | Do you use goal setting to decide what tasks and activities you should work on? |
| 7 | Do you leave contingency time in your schedule to deal with 'the unexpected'? |
| 8 | Do you know whether the tasks you are working on are high, medium or low value? |
| 9 | When you are given a new assignment, do you analyse it for importance and prioritize it accordingly? |
| 10 | Do you remain stressed about deadlines and commitments? |
| 11 | Do distractions often keep you from working on critical tasks? |
| 12 | Do you often find yourself bringing work home just to get it done? |
| 13 | Do you prioritize your 'to-do' list or action program? |
| 14 | Do you talk with your boss to prioritize the work you're doing? |
| 15 | Before you take on a task, do you check that the results will be worth the time put in? |

Identify your specific improvement areas:
**Goal Setting:** Questions 6, 10, 14, 15
**Prioritization:** Questions 1, 4, 8, 9, 13, 14, 15
**Managing Interruptions:** Questions 5, 9, 11, 12
**Procrastination:** Questions 2, 10, 12
**Scheduling:** Questions 3, 7, 12

## Summary

- Manage priorities, not time. Effectiveness versus efficiency. Identify key priorities for significant impact. Evaluate time spent on high-impact activities versus low-impact busyness. Don't be on autopilot; choose the most important roles you play.

- Manage distractions. Simplify life. Practise mind decluttering techniques like jotting down thoughts before bed or categorizing emails.

- Manage energy, not time. Understand energy drainers in personal and professional life. Embrace forgiveness and stress-relieving practices to maintain inner peace.

- Live a Quadrant II life. Not urgent but important. If we do Quadrant II well, it will automatically avoid fires in future. Address root causes to prevent recurring crises.

- Calendar management. Identify and prioritize key tasks (big rocks) each week. Things that matter most must never be at the mercy of things that matter less.

## Food for Thought: Self-Assessment

1.  Do I resonate with any of the personalities mentioned in the chapter: The Fireman (always amidst urgencies), The Yes Man (saying yes to too many things), or The Procrastinator (delaying till the pile up becomes unmanageable)? What can I do to avoid these?

2.  Am I clear on my Big Rocks—the key priorities in work and life? What are the main five to seven roles I play, and what actions can be taken in each to achieve great results and satisfaction?

3.  Am I adept at managing distractions? What specific strategies can be adopted to avoid distractions and develop focus on key goals?

4.  Do I feel drained and tired by the end of most days? What physical, mental and even spiritual behaviour changes could lead to more energy?

5.  In work and life, what specific Quadrant I (urgent and important) fires keep repeating month after month? What potential Quadrant II (not urgent

but important) activities can be pursued to reduce Quadrant I fires over time?

6.  Who controls my calendar—my colleagues or me? Do I habitually block time for things that are important? Do I regularly say no to meeting requests where the value added will be minimal?

# 6

# Accountability

'A body of men holding themselves accountable to nobody ought not to be trusted by anybody'—**Thomas Paine, French/ American revolutionary, author of *Common Sense***

'However beautiful the strategy, you should occasionally look at the results'—**Winston Churchill, former UK prime minister and hero of Second World War**

SG was a smart, cerebral and hard-working manager from a top B-school who started off as a 'high potential' employee. However, after the first few levels, his career started stagnating and he saw his peers move ahead of him. When we sat together on his feedback, we identified that most of his stakeholders would say, 'Above average intelligence but average execution.' As he himself reminiscences: 'I was solving most of the problems in my head (and assuming it done) but not really taking it forward to full execution and owning end results. I was working hard and doing my part, but the desired results were not being achieved. All this while, I was blaming reasons outside my control and playing the victim. This possibly led to a lag in career growth and me not really performing to my full potential.'

He moved on to another company, and over the next two years, worked on this feedback and is now running a large P&L and team and delivering high growth.

This habit of not taking full accountability of the outcome and blaming someone or the other is the death knell for many careers. After all, if strategy is often decided at board or CEO level and execution is done by the junior most level, then what exactly is the role of the middle layers? One big role is to take accountability of results and make sure that a promise made is a promise kept.

This mindset of accountability, unfortunately, seems to be in short supply. During my occasional teaching sessions at MBA colleges, I encounter students who are quick to attribute their actions and habits to circumstances beyond their control. A student might say, 'My father was a chain smoker, so I picked up the habit too,' as if parental influence leaves no room for personal choice. Another might explain away academic struggles with: 'My parents didn't have time for me, so I wasn't good at studies,' placing the blame squarely on their environment rather than on their own efforts. Don't get me wrong. Circumstances can create powerful influence. But they can influence, not determine. We still have the power to choose.

Take, for instance, celebrities who are offered massive paychecks to promote dubious products or endorse dubious categories. Can they justify their actions by saying, 'I'm just a paid face; I can't be held responsible for the quality of what I'm selling'? Such an excuse rings hollow. Their influence and reach come with responsibility, and shirking that responsibility undermines their credibility.

In many companies, employees are rated amazing, average or developing. Only the top 15–20 per cent are generally rated amazing. Each year, in my business, I personally interview our amazing performers. What makes them tick?

The one common theme: Accountability. Verbatim comments include '*Karna hai to bas karna hai*' [If it has to be done, it just has to be done]. They are fixated on results: 'I have to achieve targets, no matter what.' They show an ownership behaviour, 'like I am running my own business,' driving cross functional teams towards the target. They are deeply customer focussed: 'customer's voice in the company.' They display a sense of urgency: 'solving problems by picking up the phone, instead of waiting for email,' working with others to 'ensure people match my speed.'

These are the people who become indispensable because of their ability to get things done, a skill in itself. When results don't come, most people will complain, giving all kinds of genuine and not so genuine excuses. There will always be someone to blame, especially when multiple departments are involved. But eventually, what matters is that desired results were not achieved. So, where does the buck stop?

Contrary to popular belief, responsibility alone does not equate to accountability.[1] Responsibility is merely about a specific duty an individual is expected to fulfil. However, accountability takes a step further. Accountability is owning up to the end results, even if it means going above and beyond what's asked. Accountability is self-obligated whereas responsibility is assigned. A teacher's responsibility is to teach the syllabus and prepare the students for exams, but the accountability is to help the students grow by spreading wisdom. In the classroom, what separates a good teacher from a great one is the willingness to take ownership and make a real difference in students' lives.

## Good Excuse + Bad Result Is Not Equal to Good Result

A sales representative is responsible for sales but can still give excuses when sales don't happen. Supply may have been an issue, new competition gave higher discount, the market was sluggish, or the neighbouring territory stole some sales. These excuses generally claim that the individuals did everything right *within their remit*, but there were reasons *beyond their control* that explain why the end result still was not achieved.

I was frustrated. An ATM from where I withdrew money had debited my account without dispensing cash. I complained at the ATM's bank, but their account executive pleaded helplessness, saying I needed to talk to my own bank. She also did not offer any suggestion on what process was to be followed or who could be my contact.

I registered a complain at my bank. Weeks passed and nothing happened. I talked to my bank's relationship manager. She said, 'These things are handled by claims department. I can't do much about that.' When it was two months and nothing happened, I reached out to another known executive in my bank. He handled the situation very differently. 'I'm sorry to hear about this problem,' he said. 'I'll find out what happened and revert tomorrow.' Next day, he sent me a full update and promised that the concerned team will close it within three days. On the third day, I got the refund. Note this agent was not more senior than the others. If anything, he could easily have claimed he had no locus standi in this specific case.

The first two agents shirked their accountability, but the third made himself personally accountable for fixing the problem. He took ownership, apologized on behalf of his organization and helped drive outcome.

As you can see from this incident, accountable people go above and beyond. They take ownership for the end outcome, which means also for the contribution of people not directly under them. They become the glue that connects individual activities to outcome. They do not believe in playing the blame game because even if we find a good department to blame, the reality is that the results—that we were accountable for—were not achieved. We can do post-mortem and perhaps even improve processes for future, but the current project will still be called a failure, if the desired outcome is not achieved.

My company had acquired one of the largest companies in its industry in South Africa and I was relocated to Cape Town as executive director and CFO. As often happens in M&A, many of our initial assumptions at the time of acquisition were probably erroneous—the promised new launches were far from ready, the factory was bleeding, the culture was too dependent on the previous entrepreneur while everyone else worked in silos, and the integration with the parent company was not robust leading to poor supplies. In the very first year, the business delivery was miles away from budget commitment. There were murmurs of selling off and cutting losses. Our South Africa CEO called the Top 100 and said that while we can justifiably blame inherited issues, the acquisition would still be called a failure. So, blaming won't solve the problem at hand. Instead, he asked us to make a detailed plan to leverage our strengths, fix things that had gone wrong and find back-ups for the deficiencies. We were all encouraged to take additional responsibilities to cover the gaps. I personally, beyond finance, was tasked to find new products from outside that could cover up for our internal lack of pipeline and to make our local factory profitable. Coming from the India mothership, I was also tasked with integration and sorting out supplies from India. We worked on creating a culture free of silos where individuals took accountability for end results.

Long story short, over the next three years, we doubled revenues, tripled profits, doubled Return on Invested Capital (ROIC) and generally made this one of the best acquisitions by an Indian company in this industry. It is actually published as a case study in a reputed peer reviewed journal to teach post-merger integration.[2] I personally won the industry's 'Young CFO of the Year' award and both the BU CEO and I rose up within the corporate hierarchy. The message is that leaders must take full accountability, not just of specific activities but of end results. You can be pushing the wall all day long, but the wall will not move. If it is to be, it is up to me. If it is up to me, it shall be.

People who are accountable:

- Own up to end outcome, especially when results are not coming
- Avoid blaming others
- Don't like making excuses that it is all out of their control
- Connect the dots

Hence, I keep repeating to my team: Good excuse + Bad result ≠ Good result.

One of my friends, a successful venture capitalist in India, was giving the example of two of his portfolio companies during the economic slowdown. They were both at risk of going bust as fresh funding had dried out. One founder kept complaining about how investors don't understand real business and reject investments based on Microsoft Excel, that India's business climate does not support entrepreneurs, and how his great idea was unable to find funders.

The other, in a very similar situation, talked humbly about his inability to convince VCs to put more money and, therefore, the need for him to improve his pitch. And his inability to cut expenses beforehand knowing that funding could be difficult amidst overall economic challenges in the world.

The situation was similar, but one took personal accountability while the other did not. So, when this VC had to invest in a follow up round, no prizes for guessing who he put his money into.

Take a look around any college campus or government institution, and you'll notice a stark difference in how different people approach their tasks. In college, when a group assignment is handed out, you'll inevitably encounter those who constantly seek extensions, grumbling about their uncooperative teammates. Yet, amidst this chorus of complaints, there are always a few students who not only finish the task on time but also deliver good quality work—sometimes even pitching in to help their less motivated peers—all with a smile on their faces.

The same pattern emerges in the realm of politics and bureaucracy. Many ministers and civil servants find themselves mired in excuses, blaming bureaucratic red tape, budget constraints and interdepartmental conflicts for their lacklustre performance. 'It's just too difficult to get things done in this country,' they lament. At the same time, there are always a select few who stand out—the ones who refuse to be bogged down by obstacles and instead take personal accountability for driving change.

Regardless of bureaucratic hurdles, these rare individuals lead by example, rallying both their own teams and cross-functional collaborators to achieve tangible results. Their success stories span the political spectrum, from left-wing to right-wing governments, and from central to state levels. These are our prime movers.

## The Art of Execution

> 'Ideas don't move mountains, bulldozers do. Ideas just tell you where to put the bulldozers'—**Peter Drucker, management thinker, regarded as father of management**

> 'Vision without execution is hallucination'—**Thomas Edison, famous inventor**

If accountability is the right mindset, execution is the tool needed to achieve it. Without action, accountability is just an empty promise. Execution is usually the missing link between aspirations and actual results. This requires carefully linking strategy, people and operations.[3]

When someone asks me the role of a CEO, I jokingly answer: a glorified project manager. It is not a coincidence that the origin of management was on the shop floor during world war, where strategic planning—correctly deploying man, machine, money, material and method—made the difference between winners and losers.

Our job is not just to set a 'vision' and then leave others to deliver it. Strategically, we may think about wondrous growth ideas, but operationally it can all fall apart. The hallowed job of strategy formulation takes hardly a week a year, the remaining time is spent pursuing the discipline of execution. And execution must be managed, week on week, month on month, with multiple variables, multiple interdependencies and with multiple uncertainties. Like classic multivariate linear programming, this requires the science of planning. Dwight Eisenhower, the five-star general of the allied forces during world war, often recounted how successful soldiers believed in 'plans are worthless but planning is everything.' This sounds like a riddle, but it implies that whatever you plan, you may be obliged to deviate from it in response to changed circumstances on the ground. But still, the very fact that you have taken the care to think through, develop, discuss and put in place a plan, will serve you extremely well, no matter how much specific deviations you end up taking.

How exactly do star performers deliver results? Beyond the right accountability mindset, I have seen amazing performers do five things:

1.  **Advance planning:** When justifying poor monthly sales, one team complained that the customer did not place the order on time, leaving inadequate time to deliver supplies within the month. But another team (who had the same problem of late orders) still achieved their targets. They checked the customer's history to find out their ordering trends, did sales projections and kept semi-finished stock ready even before the actual purchase order. They figured out that, in the worst case, even if the order did not come within the month, it had to come in the next few months, so the built-up inventory would not go waste.

2.  **Strong follow-up:** Imagine working on a group project with teammates, each responsible for different sections. After dividing tasks and setting deadlines, you complete your portion and await input from others to integrate into the final project. However, as the deadline approaches, you notice some sections are missing. Rather than assuming

your peers will deliver on time, you send a friendly reminder email, prompting them to submit their contributions. This follow-up ensures all parts come together seamlessly and allows the group to submit a cohesive project without binging on cups of coffee before the dreaded deadline. Follow-up gets things done, ensuring balls are not getting dropped, but it also requires discipline. Some leaders hold a Monday morning call, others appoint CEO's office staff to follow up with the larger team, but all ensure that plans are actually executed. This requires some amount of detail orientation and having a pulse on each success driver. One of my former presidents used to say, 'I don't believe in micro-management, but I do believe in micro-tracking.'

Often when senior leaders come from outside, they focus mainly on the skill sets of big picture thinking and people management. But they end up undermining the importance of strong governance and regular reviews to ensure follow-ups. As a result, the future looks all bright and rosy but hard results in the near term keep lagging. Sure enough, strategy and organization are important responsibilities of leaders. But these come alive when we review the performance every week and every month, in detail, understanding the root causes when things go wrong, and holding people accountable when there is consistent under-delivery. Without getting into details and doing rigorous follow-ups, we can keep shouting and cribbing, but things will not improve.

The founder of a company I know kept saying, 'People don't do what you expect, but what you inspect, provided you do it with respect.' In these follow-ups, star performers are gentle yet firm.

3.   **Plan B:** We were moving from legacy IT system to ERP.
     Often these transitions go wrong as the new system refuses
     to talk to other applications. While eventually things get
     corrected, many precious days of sales are lost. In one such
     changeover, our project head, who refused to let Murphy's
     Law dictate the fate of this project, got everyone, including
     past implementation teams, to brainstorm all that could
     go wrong. She then divided this list of all potential failures
     into two camps: mere inconveniences and showstoppers.
     For the latter, she pushed to have a proactive plan B ready.
     And so, when the inevitable happened, and our automatic
     invoicing system decided to take an unscheduled siesta for
     twelve agonizing days, there was no panic. Our project
     manager had a backup arrangement to do manual invoicing
     and hence sales continued uninterrupted.

     In the aftermath, when the dust had settled and the
     storm clouds had parted, it would have been easy for our IT
     head to play the blame game—to point fingers and absolve
     herself of responsibility. Most people would have genuinely
     said, 'Sorry we lost sales, but it was the implementation
     team's fault, I was just the project manager.' But she took
     accountability and ensured that every potential disaster had
     a backup plan waiting in the wings.

4.   **Solution orientation:** Top performers creatively deal with
     obstacles. One of our M&A deals was stuck. The buyer had
     put a condition that our company was not willing to agree
     to. Then a middle level finance manager took the initiative
     to talk directly to the buyer, understood his concerns,
     offered a creative win-win solution and championed the
     proposal inside our company too. The deal went through
     in record time.

Just when everyone else had justifiably put the pens down citing an unreasonable buyer, this employee went above and beyond to close the deal and deliver the planned M&A. Rather than seeing the buyer's condition as a roadblock, the employee approached it as a chance to find a mutually beneficial solution.

5.  **Holding others accountable:** In an orchestra, each individual musical instrument has its own melody. The conductor knows how to make them all work together. He guides all the moving pieces, and creates music so beautiful that it draws the entire audience to the concert. Any team functions similarly.

    The fault lines often lie at the intersection of different departments. Siloed thinking takes over and everyone maximizes their specific targets instead of optimizing for the big picture. Most people explain lack of results by blaming other departments ('they were supposed to do it'). In contrast, star performers build an environment of trust, ensure free flow of information, and build strong networks across the company. They also then drive all departments, holding them accountable for the end objective while also building a relationship. Inside and outside the company, they balance empathy with strong negotiation. When needed, they escalate for help early on so action can still be taken. Not after things have already gone wrong. One of my bosses used to say, 'The difference between a problem and an excuse is that the latter comes post facto, at the month end.'

    Top performers also realize the super criticality of back-end operations and make them their ally. Indra Nooyi's successor as CEO at PepsiCo was pulled out from running their Europe business and asked to do a short stint involving operations to learn the massive back-end of PepsiCo. Only after learning that he was appointed CEO.

Holding others accounatble does not mean pointing out what went wrong. It means creating opportunities for growth. And this is where feedback becomes essential.

## Giving Feedback

Accountability and feedback go hand in hand. To inspire change, we need to master the art of delivering feedback that motivates. We need to excel in giving polite but clear feedback, understanding the psychology of the receiver. See, when people receive adverse feedback, they often experience conflicting emotions:

- First, there's the emotional response which tends to be defensive and resistant. Their ego takes over, they are upset on being corrected. This prevents the receiver from fully absorbing the content of the feedback. In fact, they see the giver as biased or having vested interests.
- After the initial emotional response, the rational part of the receiver's brain may finally get activated and it sees feedback as an opportunity for growth and improvement. They may compare the content with what they have heard in the past and try to work on it.

Good feedback givers understand that success is when feedback is actually internalized by the receiver and not just when the giver delivers the feedback. Therefore, they will try to maximize the second reaction and minimize the first.

Even before delivering feedback, establish a foundation of trust—a crucial factor in how the feedback is received. Do the recipients perceive the giver as an adversary seeking to score points, or as a genuine well-wisher intent on helping them improve? Note, it doesn't matter how the givers see themselves, only the perception of the receiver is important.

Consciously work to minimize emotional reactions. Provide negative feedback in a private setting to avoid ego hurt. And then activate the logical response. Provide specific instances and behaviour, not comment on overall personality. Give suggestions and not prescriptions. Reinforce the overall worth of the receiver.

My own manager appended difficult feedback to me like this: 'You have so much talent and are so driven. I really think you will go very far in life. I am worried that some of these correctable flaws, these little chinks in your armour, may prevent you from reaching your full potential.' I followed his advice to the hilt!

## A Culture of Accountability

Early in my career, coming from a rather technical background (engineering and then finance), I did not think much of what I fathomed were 'soft' functions like HR. And then at P&G, I saw the attrition after Gillette integration. So many ex-Gillette employees chose to leave. When I talked to them, they alluded to a big difference in company culture, from the smaller Gillette to the much bigger P&G. The left-brained me couldn't understand: P&G was a more prestigious brand name and was offering great salaries and generally a bigger role. And yet, the 'soft stuff' of culture was overshadowing all these hard benefits. This was my first awakening that culture, the shared values in a team, really ate strategy for breakfast.

For individuals to embrace accountability, companies need to create a culture that fosters accountability as a value. This involves right goal setting, right rewards, training interventions and cross-functional alignment.

Taking accountability is always more complicated in a large matrix organization where there are peers who don't report to us but whose partnership is crucial for our success. In these cases, the right organizational structure and scorecards can solve many problems.

I ran a complex business where supply was always a pain. A lot of time was spent on internal debates between commercial and supply chain—the former highlighting poor serviceability and mounting customer complaints while the latter blaming poor forecasting and long tail complexity. Simple solutions like lecturing the two teams to collaborate or doing joint reviews did not work. They were too simplistic and did not create a lasting impact. Finally, we gave the Global Supply Chain head the additional role of the management committee sponsor for this business, adding the business revenue to his scorecard. Soon a lot of noise around whose mistake it was dissipated, and the teams started focussing on end results and customer satisfaction. The right organizational structure and scorecard can solve many cross functional collaboration problems.

Conversely, business results and relationships collapse when there are misaligned expectations, especially inter-departmental. Till the above organizational change was made, there was always a fight between supply chain and commercial, which started with an issue and then engulfed the people involved. Both sides cribbed against the other and made each other's life more difficult, while the real business issues were not getting solved.

US Navy Seals, the elite crack team against terrorism, promote extreme accountability across the team. We had invited a former Navy Seal team leader to address our top team. He recounted how they employ 'buddy checks,' where each commando is paired with a 'battle buddy' to ensure mutual accountability. They regularly check each other's gear, verify readiness, and confirm the presence of essential equipment before missions. Further, Navy Seals use 'after-action reviews' (AARs) to evaluate performance post-mission. In this meeting, the team openly discusses successes, areas for improvement, and lessons learned, fostering a culture of accountability and continuous improvement. Seals operate under a decentralized command structure, where every member is empowered to take ownership of their responsibilities and make decisions within their area of expertise. This ensures accountability at all levels of the team.[4]

Accountability is about taking ownership, fostering collaboration, and driving results. It starts with the right mindset—taking ownership of outcomes, and not just of the activities. This mindset shows in work but also in our lives. We have to take final accountability of the outcomes in our lives. The opposite is to assign blame and shirk our own responsibility.

Organizations can build an entire culture of accountability, where individuals and organizations can unleash their full potential.

This also sets the stage to talk of the next skill: Collaboration.

## Summary

- Accountability means taking responsibility for achieving end results, not just completing the assigned tasks. It is about owning outcome, even if factors beyond one's direct control affect it. No excuses. No blame game.

- Every individual aspiring to leave a legacy must master the link between ideas and results. Execution bridges this gap.

- Successful execution involves advance planning, strong follow-up, backup planning, holding others accountable and being solution oriented.

- Companies can foster accountability by building the right culture. This requires working on goal setting, rewards and organizational structure.

- Personal accountability extends beyond work to life choices and behaviours. We have to own the outcomes of our life.

## Food for Thought: Self-Assessment

1. Do I find myself merely fulfilling responsibilities assigned to me, or am I actively taking ownership of achieving desired outcomes, even in situations where I may not have direct control? Do others perceive me as someone who goes above and beyond?

2. Am I adept at advance planning and diligent follow-up, ensuring that tasks are not just assigned but successfully completed with attention to detail and accountability?

3. How do my actions and communication contribute to a culture of accountability and ownership within the team or organization? Do I hold others accountable, gently yet firmly?

4. When faced with a hurdle, do I try to find a creative yet practical solution? Or do I go to my manager with the belief that the situation is at a standstill.

5. Do I genuinely take ownership of both my successes and failures, without shifting blame onto external factors?

6.  For important projects, do I actively create a plan B
    and even a plan C just in case the main plan goes awry?

# 7

## Collaboration

'Your corn is ripe today; mine will be so tomorrow. 'Tis profitable for us both, that I should labour with you today, and that you should aid me tomorrow'—**David Hume, Scottish enlightenment philosopher**

'We may have all come on different ships, but we're in the same boat now'—**Martin Luther King Jr., American civil rights leader**

We all intuitively know and acknowledge the significance of collaboration. Maybe we were mandated to attend that tiresome seminar on collaboration where we find ourselves daydreaming about lunch while someone passionately preaches the virtues of working together. Or maybe it all boils down to common sense: Homo sapiens are 'social animals'; we are wired to thrive on social interaction and connection.

However, what is common sense does not necessarily translate to common practice. No different from how we know we should exercise regularly, but the allure of the couch and the TV remote is just too strong.

UP used to run my CEO office. He was an entrepreneurial go-getter, always looking at opportunities, and finding ways to get things done. Impressed, I moved him to running an independent, complex P&L. The first year was successful— he found new product opportunities and new customers, and business grew. However, in the course of his work, he started pushing too hard many cross functional leaders—supply, quality, finance, legal, regulatory—whom he considered were slowing him down and impacting business performance. His concerns were real but instead of reconciling those differing views, every meeting became a finger pointing blame-game. This resulted in real issues remaining unsolved and business started stagnating next year.

As his mentor, I tried to give him feedback. But despite his brilliance, this trait of 'my way or the highway' was just too deeply engrained in him. He would try and make amends but very quickly revert to his original style. A part of him was not convinced he had a role to play in the poor collaboration. His superiors and subordinates loved his passion, but his peers found him immature. Eventually, both of us felt a large corporate hierarchy would not get the best out of him. He left his reputed, high paying job and recently started his own venture.

Even the smartest of the smart need to enhance the skill of collaboration. Without it, we won't go very far, at least in a large matrix organization. These require working with and through people to build a unified team. Collaboration becomes even more complicated when we have to influence peers who don't report to us but are critical for our success. A consulting friend told me that consultants are rated by peers in other practices for their main role is to influence without the benefit of authority.

Companies and societies are inherently interdependent, meaning one person's success is rarely achieved without the support of others. One can lead a happy married life only if other members of the family are also happy. Similarly, a project succeeds only if all colleagues give full support. In my Cape Town days, I encountered the word Ubuntu from Zulu language which means 'I am, because we are.' We are interconnected. This African wisdom of collective living is not very different from the Indian concept of 'vasudhaiv kutumbhkum,' the whole world is a family.[1]

Thomas Malone, professor of management at MIT Sloan school, makes this insightful statement: 'If you're like most people, you probably believe that humans are the most intelligent animals on our planet. But there's another kind of entity that can be far smarter: groups of people.'[2] Almost all our discoveries and successes—whether in the military, healthcare or organizations—have emerged from collective effort. No wonder then good organizations put a premium on collaborative skills.

I had a personal awakening when I was posted in India as the deputy CFO of P&G India. This was the year P&G had acquired Gillette, and we had delivered some breakthrough results. However, my annual performance assessment—usually always at the top—came out average. My CEO took me aside and explained that in the desire to push results, I had developed rough edges and insecurities that were making collaboration difficult. He shared feedback from others who complimented my strengths but also pointed out it was not easy to work with me. While at that time I felt angry and upset, later, on deeper introspection, I realized there were incidents when to save my own reputation, I had not taken full ownership and passed blame to others. When there was a conflict, I would focus on advancing my point of view and took less genuine interest in understanding the other person. This was probably the best wake up call I could have had. And since then, I came to be known as an organization builder and a magnet for talent. A lot of this change came through the steps recounted below.

I have personally known and mentored some promising individuals. They possess the capability—passion, knowledge and skills—necessary to get the job done. However, they are often remiss in one area and cannot reach their full potential. The missing ingredient is that they lack the maturity required to collaborate effectively.

We had a leadership presentation by a former US Navy SEAL, the elite commando unit in the United States of America. He spoke as much about group collaboration and trust as he spoke about individual fitness and training. Commando units rely on each other to cover their backs, watch out for threats and provide critical support. There's the sniper providing cover, the medic ready to patch up injuries, the strategist making critical decisions, and the support personnel keeping the team supplied. If any one of them fails to collaborate effectively, the entire mission could crumble. 'One for all, all for one,' the presenter kept emphasizing. The stakes are literally life and death.[3]

Yet, the same quality of collaboration is not as common in corporate. Research conducted by *Harvard Business Review*, spanning more than 300 organizations, revealed that a mere 3 per cent to 5 per cent of employees contribute to a staggering 20 per cent to 35 per cent of value-added collaborations.[4]

What about most of the others? Why is it so hard? Because again, we first need to start with the right mindset.

## The Mindset: Abundance vs Scarcity

I lived in Gurgaon and then in Cape Town. One thing that intrigued me was how traffic evolved at junctions without traffic lights, where commuters had to self-regulate. In Gurgaon, it was a race to the finish, with everyone wanting to go first, resulting in a very avoidable and frustrating jam. No one wanted to let the other person get through. In contrast, in the well-to-do suburbs of Cape Town, motorists would give a signal with their finger to the other person to get through based on who reached the junction first. And largely, there was a smooth and orderly flow even without any external supervision.

I asked a psychologist friend why two sets of people would behave so differently, and she directed me to Covey's work on abundance and scarcity mindset.[5] Since the suburbs of Cape Town had abundant land area and limited cars, over many decades, the citizens started believing that there was plenty of physical space for everyone, and they wouldn't lose by letting the other person go first. However, in much of urban North India, where overpopulation meets limited space, motorists have learned that there isn't enough room for everyone. Those who get ahead may pass through, while the rest remain stuck in an endless-seeming queue. Hence the game of one upmanship.

Now obviously, this explanation is simplistic. Other factors like rule enforcement play a role too but this is still illustrative of how our mindset governs our behaviour.

People with an abundance mentality believe there is plenty for everyone, including themselves and others. Their behaviour then automatically becomes more giving and sharing. On the other hand, people with a scarcity mindset believe resources are limited and one must compete for a share. With such an outlook, they end up not collaborating. Hence, Covey suggested that before anything else we need to develop an abundance mindset.

The important thing is that this mentality helps us, even if resources aren't truly abundant. For example, there is only one CEO in an organization, so in that sense, the career opportunity for the N-1 layer can be called scarce. But if we spend too much time worrying that resources are limited, we end up getting insecure, jealous, impatient and overall negative. Instead of focusing on performing well, we also start wanting to pull the other person down. In good organizations, this behaviour gets noticed and takes us down as well, at least in the long run. An abundance mentality, on the other hand, makes us generous, freely sharing and genuinely happy in the success of others, bringing us a wealth of positive vibes. Not to mention we become a happier person, which is perhaps even more important than winning.

My father recounted this incident from the 1960s when he was a young man, full of ideas and eager to create change. Unfortunately, he lived in this slum in a large house where all our relatives stayed together in a traditional joint family. There were many fun moments but also a lot of, shall we say, family politics, with often people spending time talking about one another and wanting to bring the other's reputation down. These emanated from the family matriarch, my taiji (aunt), a strong-willed widow with a penchant to discipline anyone who wouldn't listen to her. And my father was getting stuck in the mess—getting involved in a new minor crisis every day. One day he went to my taiji and said, 'We can keep playing this game, just know that I am young, and you are old, and I will eventually win. But my life will also get ruined in this well. Instead, let me focus on my career and a life outside this slum. I promise if I am successful, I will take care of you too.' Something in the way he said or what he said appealed to her. And from that day, she became my father's biggest supporter, helping him focus, shielding him from all the family drama. In a few years, my father became a lawyer and moved to an urban neighbourhood where I was born. Amongst his dozen siblings, he was probably the only one to have moved ahead in life. And till her last day, taiji would visit us and get a lot of respect and love from us and give us a lot of love too.

So, every fight is not worth fighting. Pick your battles.

## The Thinking: Win-Win

I spent quite some time in M&A and earned accolades on closing deals. [Though admittedly, whether all these deals did well over the next few years is all together a different story]. My mantra was simple. Never focus on splitting the pie, because then whatever I try and get necessarily reduces the share of the other side. Instead, let's focus on growing the pie, creating more overall value together. Then I was happily willing to share an extra part of this increased value with the other side. Their win did not mean my loss. And so, we were able to create deal structures that worked for both sides. For instance, I would offer a base valuation based on my team's projections (which was usually lower than the other side's expectations) but then be willing to have additional payouts if stretch profits were achieved over the next five years.

The moment we frame negotiation in mutually exclusive terms (i.e., their win must mean my loss), collaboration is impossible. We may still win short term if our bargaining position is strong but would lose the larger relationship and our ability to keep winning in future. In fact, sometimes, strategically, we may want to lose an argument just to preserve an important relationship. Ask any parent.

Win-win thinking involves discovering a genuine synergy where the combined efforts result in higher benefits than the sum of individual contributions, i.e., $1+1=3$. In contrast, compromise often leads to a situation where one or both parties give up something, i.e., a compromise is $1+1=1.5$. If spouses are having a fight over whether to go for a movie or to go for shopping, and one relents and agrees to go with the other's choice, that is a compromise. It is probably better than fighting with each other, but not healthy in the long run since the one who ends up making the sacrifice will start feeling he/she is giving more than getting, and harbour resentment. Finding a better creative alternative—better than either movie or shopping alone and that excites both parties—is at the heart of win-win. It could be watching a movie in a shopping mall or discovering a new activity like strolling by the sea. Literally both sides have to say, we will keep brainstorming till we find an alternative that makes us both happy—a true win-win.

As you can imagine, win-win thinking, actively working to ensure our partner achieves their desired win knowing that it is the only sustainable way for us to get our win too and that both can happen together, will not happen till we first have an abundance mindset. The mindset that there is enough and more in the world for both of us to get what we want.

Note also that giving in, accepting the other side's view just to keep them happy, is also not win-win. It is not sustainable. We will be resentful and keep cribbing and subconsciously not let the other side enjoy their win too.

## Empathetic Listening

My career started with P&G Japan. After my very first business meeting, my manager asked me what it was about and I explained it was an induction where a brand manager was trying to orient me into the local business. Her response was gentle yet impactful, 'The goal was for you to learn, but I saw through the meeting room window that you were doing most of the talking!' It was a moment of realization for me. As articulate and confident Indians, we often fall in love with our own voice and fail to listen. The Japanese, on the other hand, are masters in the art of empathy and listening. They skillfully absorb perspectives with a sincerity that struck me.

Listening is still easier when both sides are wanting the same thing. But when there is difference of opinion, we hardly try to listen with empathy. Out of politeness, we may still maintain a facade of listening, but aren't we crafting our own rebuttal inside our heads?

Empathetic listening suggests we put ourselves in the speaker's shoes. For a while, can we suspend our own biases and judgment and genuinely try to understand why an equally intelligent person has a view that, at first glance, seems different from ours. Listening does not mean agreeing or disagreeing, just suspending judgement and understanding. Unfortunately, while our education system offers many classes on reading, writing and speaking, it largely neglects the skill of listening. So, we grow up to be great speakers and writers but poor listeners—making collaboration, both in professional and personal lives, difficult.

And yet, the wisdom of putting ourselves in the other person's shoes is timeless. 'Acquire the habit of listening carefully to what is being said by another, and of entering, so far as possible, into the mind of the speaker,' said the wise emperor Marcus Aurelius in *Meditations* nearly two thousand years ago.

Perhaps the gold standard on empathetic listening is the 'speaker's staff.'[6] This unassuming tool has its origins in Native American culture where it played a role in preventing conflicts and war. Imagine a time when tribes faced disputes that could easily escalate into war since each tribal lord had the power to command a small army. The 'speaker's staff' came to the rescue. Before a tribal leader could commit his troops into war, the two warring chieftains had to sit together. Whoever held the staff had the floor and others were bound by an unwritten agreement to listen without interruption. The staff was then passed to the other side but *only* when the first side confirmed they *felt* understood. Meaning the listening side had to prove— through eye contact, body language, rephrasing of content and summarizing—that they had indeed understood the speaker's point of view as clearly as the speaker. Understanding does not mean agreeing, just that they know where the speaker was coming from. Then the other side made their points while the first listened. Not just a show of listening but deeply engaged listening since the staff wouldn't come back unless the speaker felt understood. Over few iterations, most misunderstandings were resolved.

The Chinese language uses symbols instead of alphabets. The word for listening includes the symbols for ear, eyes and heart—ancient reminder that all three faculties have to be engaged for good listening. Empathetic listening is not just about hearing words; it goes beyond the mere physiological process of sensation where the auditory nerve carries the impulse to register in the brain. Empathetic listening internalizes the speaker's thoughts and emotions, understanding what may not be actually said, thus gaining an insight into their perspective.

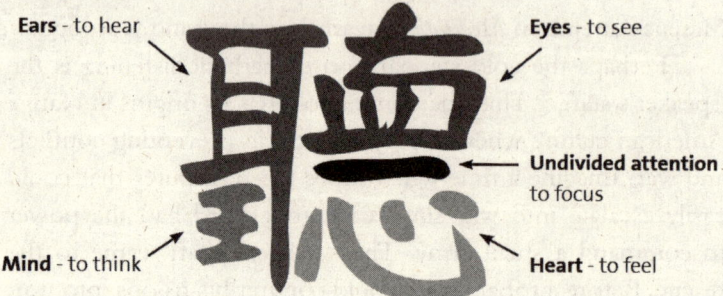

**Ears** - to hear  
**Eyes** - to see  
**Undivided attention** to focus  
**Mind** - to think  
**Heart** - to feel

# Ladder Of Inference

Another tool I found interesting was one I saw in use at Cadbury while consulting with them. It is called the Ladder of Inference (see picture below), and is a metaphor for how every inference we draw or the belief that we hold is rooted in some data that we saw but then spiced up with our own biases, interpretations and assumptions.[7]

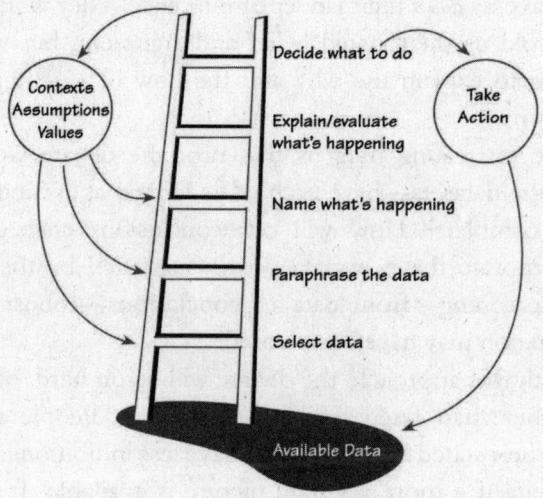

We start with seeing some data. Data, in itself, is neutral and devoid of biases. But then as we interpret this data, each one of us applies our unique lenses. We infuse the selected data with meaning, integrating personal experiences and beliefs. Wherever the data is incomplete, we subconsciously introduce assumptions to construct a framework for our understanding. We draw final conclusions, forming opinions and judgments. Ostensibly, this is based on the data we saw, but in reality, it is also rooted in our interpretations and assumptions. Over time, sustained opinions become beliefs—guiding principles that inform our actions.

This process of moving from our observations to our beliefs is like climbing a ladder with raw data at the bottom and our beliefs at the top.

Whenever there is a difference of opinion, the invitation is to take the other person *up* our ladder of inference. Meaning, instead of debating on our conclusion and belief, we explain what data we saw, how we interpreted it and, based on that, what opinions we now harbour. Then we encourage the other side to take us *down* their ladder of inference. They would have already told us their stated belief and argument, but we now ask them to explain the why and the how of reaching those conclusions.

The interesting thing is that now the debate would be around the datasets—have each of us looked at accurate data? Was it complete? How will our conclusions change when we incorporate the new data points suggested by the other? Is the reasoning—from data to conclusions—robust or the interpretation may have been biased?

With this approach, the debate will be on hard, objective data rather than fixed beliefs or opinions. People tend to protect their stated beliefs but will have less inhibition in giving up on data if a more accurate picture is available. It's about questioning our interpretations, challenging our assumptions and seeking diverse perspectives. It's about building bridges instead of walls.

## Case Study

In the *Timeless Skills* workshop, we did a role play to demonstrate win-win thinking and empathetic listening. Three volunteers were chosen at random to step into the shoes of a fictional family. The scene is set as a young daughter arriving very late from a party with friends while the concerned parents are waiting nervously at home. The cast of characters include the concerned father, the agitated mother and the oblivious young daughter.

We ask the volunteers and the group to immerse into the mindset of a parent. Feel the heart race as parents anxiously await the daughter's return from a late-night party, worried whether she was safe or not. Then picture the spirited young daughter, her enthusiasm tinged with rebellion, as she strolls in, oblivious to the storm brewing. From here on, the volunteers were free to speak as they felt. Below is the transcript from an actual session where three senior employees were playing these roles impromptu.

## Scene 1: The Initial Enactment

[The setting is a living room in a typical family home. The concerned parents, say Mr and Mrs Gupta, are nervously awaiting their daughter's return. The daughter walks in late from a party.]

Mr Gupta (authoritative and stern): Do you have any idea what time it is? We have been worried! Why did you not call?

The daughter (defensively): My phone battery died.

Mrs Gupta (accusingly): You've crossed all boundaries. This is unacceptable!

The daughter (feeling cornered): Mom, Dad, I'm twenty. I need some independence to live life my way. I can't remain a child forever.

Mr Gupta (unyielding): We don't need excuses. You need to learn responsibility.

The daughter (feeling frustrated): But I am responsible, and all my friends were there. Returning at 10 p.m. is not a big deal in today's age.

Mrs Gupta (pedantically): We are saying all this for your own safety only. Don't you know Delhi is unsafe for girls late in the evening.

The daughter (exasperatedly starts walking towards her room): And yet, here I am safe and sound. When have you guys ever listened to my view!

We take a break here for de-brief. I asked the daughter if she felt understood, and she said no. I asked the parents whether they felt the daughter had really understood their concerns. They said no too. So, this discussion became an argument, and no real solution emerged. Because there was no real listening, each side prepared their response as they feigned 'listening.' The concerned parents and their daughter faced off in a classic 'me against you' scenario. Their conflicting interests regarding the daughter's safety and independence seemed like an unsolvable equation. Worse, the relationship also broke down.

Differences, when allowed to linger without closure, move subtly from the issue to the person. We start with saying we don't like the other person's views. Very soon, it morphs into —we don't like the other person.

As the facilitator, I highlighted the lack of progress and encouraged the participants to try empathetic listening. For a moment, drop their biases and deeply try to understand the view of the other side. Why does their dear daughter, who they themselves have raised, have a view so different from theirs? What perspective are they missing? Likewise for the daughter— is there a way where the parents' anxiety can be reduced without compromising on her independence? The aim is to try and find a win-win creative solution. The role play commences again.

## Scene 2: Revisiting the Scenario with Empathetic Listening

Mr Gupta (softly with understanding): Do you have any idea what time it is? We've been worried.

Mrs Gupta (gently): We care about you, sweetie. Can you tell us what happened tonight?

The daughter (feeling heard): Mom, Dad, I lost track of time at the party. I'm really sorry for making you worry.

Mr Gupta: We understand that it can happen. Let's talk about how we can avoid this in the future.

Mr Gupta: We were worried, but we also want you to enjoy your social life and be safe. How can we balance your independence with our concerns for your well-being?

Mrs Gupta (supportively): Yes, sweetie, let's work together to find a solution that keeps you safe and allows you reasonable independence.

The daughter (feeling included): Thanks, Mom and Dad. Maybe we can set some reasonable time limit and communication rules that work for all of us.

Mr Gupta: Can I pick you up if you are getting late? Just send me the coordinates twenty to thirty minutes before.

The daughter: Hmm. Sometimes. But this may not always be possible. What if I am coming with a friend whom you also know and trust?

Mrs Gupta: We could live with that, as long as it is in a car and the person is known to us. And the driver is not drunk!

The daughter (laughing): Okay settled then!

Both parties involved in an argument may have differences of views at a shallow level. But in an interdependent reality, at a deeper level, the success of both lies in the same thing. If we frame the conflict as mutually exclusive, collaboration becomes impossible—the daughter wants the freedom to stay out late like her friends, while the parents insist on a strict 10 p.m. deadline. Only one can win and the other loses against their stated position.

But if you delve deeper beyond the superficial squabble, what the parents want is safety of the child. The 10 p.m. deadline is just a stated position to ensure that. On this deeper concern of safety, there is no conflict with the daughter who obviously also wants her safety. Similarly, the daughter wants to be independent and confident with an active friend circle. Again, this is something most parents will have no objection to—in fact, they will encourage it for healthy mental and emotional development of the child. So, while we are fighting, the irony is that at a deeper level we both want the same things. Then it is about creative win-win solutioning that delivers both. Both sides continue to brainstorm till they find a solution that ensures both the needs of safety and independence are met, and not only just one side's needs. Then the discussion is not me vs you, but me and you vs the problem.

I have seen throughout my career that win-win solutioning and empathetic listening are a recipe for resolving conflicts, whether in a family or in the boardroom. Arguments are about emotions and ego while discussion is about ideas and solutions. This is a big shift in mindset. In arguments, like in a court room, our goal is to find newer and newer logical statements to help us win. On the other hand, in a true discussion, say in a meeting to design a product, we strive to find a higher solution, building on each other's perspective and not stopping till everyone feels the solution is better than what we started with.

## Watch Out: The Paradox of Excessive Collaboration

Like everything in life, strive for the optimal level. Collaboration is obviously great, but too much of it can also lead to loss of individuality. And take a lot of time.

Research suggests the time spent by both managers as well as employees in collaborative activities has escalated by an astonishing 50 per cent or more.[8] It is an enormous acceleration that deserves applause, but it also beckons us to pause and think.

Most of our time today is spent in meetings, responding to the constant stream of requests from colleagues. There's barely a moment to catch our breath for solitary work. This doesn't leave much room for imagination and productivity. Excessive collaboration, although well-intentioned, can lead to diminished productivity and employee burnout.

After two years as general manager, I started keeping my Friday calendar free. Unless you were the managing director of the entire company, it was very difficult to get meeting time with me on a Friday. The day was dedicated solely to thinking— about new launches, strategic priorities, people, trainings, external benchmarking, self-learning and self-rejuvenation. I also tried to slot a date lunch with my wife once a week, usually Fridays. If I wanted to discuss ideas with someone, I would spontaneously call one on one to discuss, instead of setting up a pre-arranged meeting.

This balance of quiet time with collaboration time is crucial, not just on Fridays but every day. In my quest to try to achieve this balance, I stumbled upon an unexpectedly hilarious solution: I started the healthy habit of drinking a minimum of two litres of water a day. Our office boy would put a water bottle on my desk every morning and I would make it a point to not leave the office till I finished it. One obvious consequence of this was the need to go to the loo very often, as my bladder declared mutiny every couple of hours. Initially, I found this interruption disruptive but then it became a welcome break between meetings. I would finish one discussion, and in the five-minute walk to the rest room and back, clear my head, consolidate my core take-aways, and get mentally ready for the next meeting. Health and sanity together with these five-minute breaks from the corporate grind.

The other danger of excessive collaboration is conformity, the primitive human tendency to comply. This includes anything from reluctantly nodding in agreement with another department's proposal to sidestepping potential fallout by avoiding the dreaded 'no,' or discreetly keeping one's hand lowered in a meeting to avoid the risk of being the lone dissenter.

A study[9] aimed to answer the question: Will the participants in an experiment conform to group consensus, keeping aside their own opinions and judgment? They presented a line segment and tasked the participants with selecting the matching line from a set of three segments (A, B and C), each with varying lengths.

The experimenter individually quizzed each participant about their choice. Sometimes, the entire group converged on the correct answer. But occasionally, the group collectively veered off course, insisting that a different line is a true match when it was not.

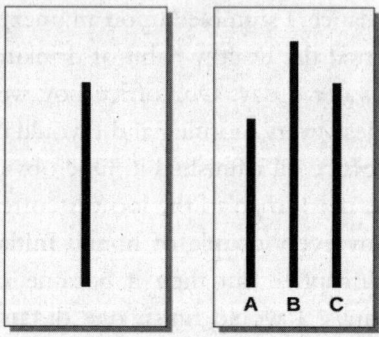

We would think that people would stick to their 'correct answer' irrespective of what the rest of the group was saying. But the research revealed that nearly 75 per cent of participants in conformity experiments, at some point, yielded to group consensus and went along with the group's wrong answer. Even if the correct answer in the picture given above is clearly C, the participant would compliantly go along with the wrong answer (say A) if everyone else in the room did. Some participants were interviewed later after they were debriefed about the experiment. They disclosed that their inclination to conform stemmed from an aversion to being the outlier or being the odd one out, even if they recognized that they were providing an incorrect response. The fear of standing out or challenging the status quo can inadvertently lead to an excess of conformity. This will inhibit creative breakthroughs and breed complacency.

Now, pair this newfound insight of how people tend to conform, whether intentionally or unintentionally, with India's deeply ingrained collectivist culture, and we can see how 'excessive collaboration' can sneak up in the workplace. [For those interested to explore this more, watch the highly acclaimed courtroom drama *Ek Ruka Hua Faisla* (1986), inspired by *12 Angry Men* (1957).]

So, how do we walk the tightrope between personal creativity and group cooperation, and navigate that elusive boundary between individuality and unity? Balance is the key, not easy and not a clear metric. Learning the art of discerning when to engage in conflicts and when to embrace collaboration is a hallmark of effective managers. Which is probably why management is an art and a science. This topic of balance—not just in deciding the optimal level of collaboration but generally in life—is elaborated upon throughout the next chapter.

# Summary

- Collaboration is the bedrock for success, especially in large matrix organizations. Because the reality we live in is interdependent, meaning we cannot be successful without the other person's full support.
- Collaboration Mindset: Abundance vs Scarcity
  - Abundance: There is plenty in the world so giving to others will not hamper our own chances.
  - Scarcity: If I give to you, I will have less.
  - Abundance mindset promotes giving and sharing while scarcity mindset leads to competition and lack of collaboration.
- Collaboration Thinking: Win-Win
  - Focus on growing the pie rather than splitting it
  - Synergy (1+1=3) and not compromise (1+1=1.5).
  - Giving in and sulking is not win-win. It is not sustainable.
- Collaboration Behaviour: Empathetic Listening
  - Listen with heart, eyes and ears. Listen to what is not said.
  - Wrong behaviour is to listen with an intent to reply, practising our response in our head while putting up a façade of listening.
  - Speaker's Staff: Suspend biases and genuinely try to understand the other's perspective. We don't speak till the other person *feels* understood.

- o  Ladder of Inference: Take others up our ladder (from the data we saw to the conclusions we drew). Ask them to take us down their ladder of inference (why are they saying what they are saying).
- o  Not me vs you, but me and you together vs the problem.
- The Paradox of Excessive Collaboration
- o  With all the benefits of collaboration, watch out against excessive collaboration, which can lead to conformity and suboptimal productivity.
- o  Recognize when to engage in conflicts and when to collaborate.

## Food for Thought: Self-Assessment

1.  Have I ever found myself in a situation where my passion and desire for speed clashed with the need for collaboration? How did I handle it and what did I learn from this experience?

2.  Think about a difficult negotiation at the office where even after repeated discussions, an agreement is still not reached. How can I adopt an abundance mindset and prioritize creating value for both parties (win-win) over securing my own interests?

3.  Think about a conflict at home where my perspective is different from other stakeholders. How do I then listen empathetically? What barriers may be preventing me from truly understanding others' point of view? How can the ladder of inference be used to bring them up from data to conclusions?

4.  Can the same be done (#3) for an unresolved conflict at work, by listening empathetically instead of listening to respond?

5. Considering the dangers of excessive collaboration, have I ever experienced a situation where conformity hindered creative thinking or decision-making? How can the need for collaboration then be balanced with maintaining one's individuality?

6. Reflecting on the example of traffic behaviour in Gurgaon and Cape Town, how does my environment influence my collaborative mindset? What changes can be made to foster a more collaborative culture?

# 8

# Balance

'Half of me is filled with bursting words and half of me is painfully shy. I crave solitude yet also crave people. I want to pour life and love into everything yet also nurture my self-care and go gently. I want to live within the rush of primal, intuitive decision, yet also wish to sit and contemplate. This is the messiness of life—that we all carry multitudes, so must sit with the shifts. We are complicated creatures, and ultimately, the balance comes from this understanding'— **Victoria Erikson, author of *Edge of Wonder***

'Balance is not something you find, it's something you create'—**Jana Kingsford, author of *Unjuggled***

GM was an accomplished manager: ambitious, articulate, hard-working and rightly prided herself on being an achiever. She was strong willed, raised a child as a single mother and persevered despite all naysayers. She also had a great executive presence and would network extensively with senior leaders. She had the wonderful skill of fully understanding her managers' needs and making their priority her own and deliver great quality work with a sense of urgency. Sure enough, she rose quickly till middle management.

However, her ambition, once her asset, began to be over bearing. What had once been seen as drive now came across as impatience and demanding. She started asking for promotion as a right with a subtle undertone of resignation if her ask was not met. In the first instance, the company caved in but then everyone started wondering if she was becoming 'too high maintenance,' and whether the emotional drain to retain her was worth the reward.

Meanwhile, as the years ticked by, her urgency only intensified. The CXO chair loomed in her mind and so she started comparing herself with every individual, inside and outside the company, who had done better than her. But instead of using their success for motivation, she chose the sour grapes route, attributing their rise to favouritism, luck, or any reason except merit. When met with criticism, she started picking fights with her manager. Instead of introspecting, she viewed herself as the victim and complained that the company was biased. The fine line between determination and obstinacy had started to blur—many others started seeing her as full of herself, more interested in her own growth than that of the business or team around her. Despite her undeniable talent, her career hit a speed bump. Sensing this, I tried to offer some feedback—her greatest strength was at risk of becoming a limitation, and she needed to find a balance. However, having witnessed success throughout her life by being ambitious and pushing her case aggressively, she now struggled to perceive it as a liability. On the contrary, in her dictionary, being diplomatic was merely a polite way of being manipulative. Unfortunately, she was denied a promotion that she felt she deserved and left to join a much smaller business.

Balance. Such a simple, understated word. And yet so crucial in life and work. People have strengths, and over the years they see how much this strength contributes to their success. Then they start leaning towards it to the point of overdoing it. And beyond a point, the same strength becomes a weakness.

To be fair to the individual, the 'right' balance is elusive and difficult. First, it is driven by the specific context. For example, some bosses will accept and celebrate greater aggression than others. Some situations demand greater aggression than other situations. Second, good results often mask many sins and thus for a long while our off-balance may remain undetected. As a result, often, the individual does not really get a clear, consistent signal on how urgent the need to improve is. And therefore, continues to exhibit old behaviour. Third, the concept of balance—pursuing a goal only to an optimal point and then stopping just before we are overdoing it—is itself vague. Till when is aggression good to drive results and when exactly does it start getting detrimental?

And yet, in other spheres of life, we effortlessly strike a balance every day. Think about our physical existence. We all know how well our bodies maintain the balance required for survival under changing external environments, in a self-regulating process called homeostasis. Beads of perspiration appear when the sun turns up the heat, maintaining a balance to cool down. Or goosebumps form when a cold wave hits us (small muscles contract producing heat). The salt we put in our meals, and even the act of walking itself, is contingent on this principle of balance. And yet, we forget this primordial lesson in our day-to-day behaviour.

In philosophy, too, we hear a lot about balance, especially in the Eastern context. The Chinese Yin and Yang symbol or taijitu shows balance between two opposites—Yin is the female, dark, cold energy and Yang symbolizes the masculine, light, warm energy. Similarly, the entire Tao philosophy from fourth century BCE is centred around the achievement of 'the Way' that finds harmony and balance within us. Buddhism talks of the Middle Way without succumbing to extremes. Buddha initially lived a princely life centred around sensual pleasures but got bored. Then he tried the other extreme of rigorous asceticism that punished his body but soon realized it was futile too in giving him peace. He finally recommended a balanced life, the Buddhist Middle Way.

But balance in the corporate world is not talked about enough and is often overlooked. Ironic, since 'and' thinking, as opposed to 'or' thinking, is crucial in business. We need revenue growth, profits *and* compliance, not either/ or. We need to deliver short term *and* long term results, since the first drives accountability while the other drives health. We need to hold our team accountable *and* keep them inspired—finding the balance without being too hard or too soft.

Let us consider some examples.

## Balance Between Confidence and Empathy

On the one hand, managers need the courage to articulate their proposals, make tough decisions and take calculated risks. It's about confidently leading the project forward. On the other, understanding involves actively listening to team members, appreciating their differing perspectives, and recognizing the limitations of our own viewpoint. Only exhibiting the former behaviour will drive speed of execution but with serious rough edges that will antagonise everyone else and become unsustainable. Only the latter behaviour will drive collaboration but slow down decision making and carry the risk of things not getting done. We need a balance between pushing our views and genuinely appreciating other views.

While simple, as the real-life example above showed, it is very rare for a person to be both an articulate speaker and an equally good listener. Great speakers often fall in love with their own voice and develop blind spots that everyone can see but not them because they are so full of themselves. On the other hand, sometimes very empathetic people start caring so much about what others are thinking that they stop being clear of what they want to achieve. They follow the path of least resistance—affable and well-liked but unwilling to challenge popular opinion.

Those few who are able to balance both adorn the highest offices. They possess the courage to articulate their own point of view as well as the empathy to understand the other person's point of view. In psychology, the term used is assertiveness: being self-assured and confident to defend the right point of view but without being aggressive.[1] It can be learned.

## Balance Between Challenging and Nurturing

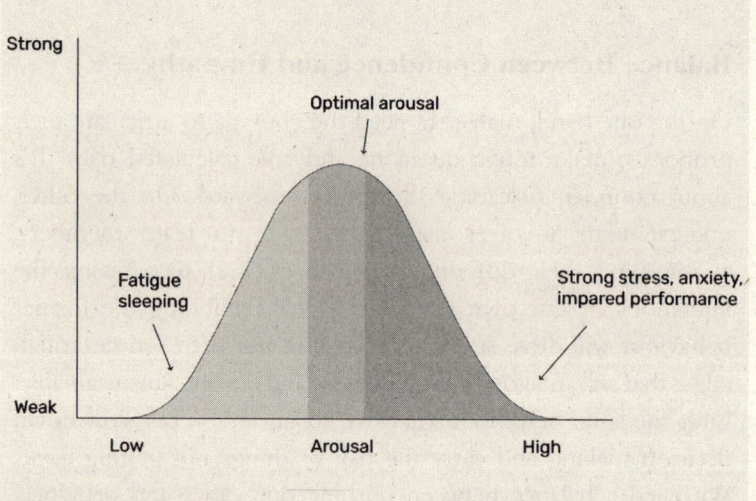

**Source:** Wikimedia Commons

Carefully regard the graph positioned above with performance on one axis and stress on the other. The Yerkes-Dodson Law,[2] originating from the early twentieth century, maps out this relationship proposing that there is an optimal level of stress/ challenge for peak performance. Too little makes people lethargic and uninspired while too much creates burnout.

In one of my CEO roles, with a couple of resignations in my team, I realized my own leadership flaws:

- With all the right intent to help my team improve, sometimes I pushed them so hard with negative feedback that I pushed them away. I thought I was being constructive, but they interpreted it as me not having their back.
- I was challenging them too much on what could be done better instead of celebrating and leveraging what my team member was already doing well.

I wanted to correct this flaw but the change for me was not easy. I tried to be more nurturing, but then I overcorrected, and became 'too soft.' My HR quipped I was procrastinating on people decisions and accepting mediocre performance. I was not holding people accountable and had started to do their job for them. In other words, I was trying to be too nice.

In fact, in one large study reported in *Harvard Business Review* involving 5400 high-level managers, 46 per cent were rated poorly on the measure 'Holds people accountable—firm when they don't deliver.'[3]

Ironically, we had a different general manager who perhaps leaned heavily on the side of extracting results. He gave stretch targets, monitored the numbers aggressively, made it clear that people had to solve their own problems, and reduced interaction with N-2 layer. In this case, the discipline and rigour were high, but the business lost multiple top performers.

Blake and Mouton popularized the 9.9 leadership model.[4] High concern for people (shown by 9-score on a 9-point scale) and equally high concern for results. Delivering only one is easy. Inspiring people *while* holding them accountable for results requires balance and maturity. Balancing empathy for their circumstances while still holding some stubbornness for results. The right balance where we are neither too soft nor too hard on our people. Neither too accommodative, nor too exacting.

We all want to be fair, meaning impartial, non-discriminative and reasonable. But fairness does not mean being nice. A lot of people will be unhappy when we make a tough call. One of my bosses used to say, 'If you cannot take hard calls on people, don't make friends at work.'

In the real world, every employee is a mixed bag, and it requires a balanced judgement to decide how much to push them to improve and how much to accept their flaws. Over time, I have come to believe that if there is innate talent and an openness to learn, we should lean on the side of helping employees improve instead of always critiquing them. On the other hand, if it is clear that we are beating a dead horse (either because of capability issue or just a misfit versus requirement), it is better to take hard calls early than prolonging the inevitable and losing productivity. Be clear of the principles and announce them upfront. While we drive hard messages in groups, use the magic of one-on-ones to ensure motivation and loyalty.

The dilemma between challenging and nurturing plays out every day in our families too. How much do we challenge our kids to become the best they can be? After all, isn't reaching our fullest potential the classic definition of success. But this path to eventual success will be strewn with difficulties and our kids will occasionally fall. Hostel life will be lonely, making new friends will be difficult, there will be nostalgia for the comfort of home, especially when they are sick, teachers would be difficult and occasionally rude, coursework will be tough and boring, job search will be taxing. At what stage do we jump in to support and nurture? As loving parents, we would want to help avoid any suffering to our kids. But then we forget that this suffering builds character. Let me again quote the founder of Nvidia: 'Greatness comes from character. And character isn't formed out of smart people, it's formed out of people who suffered.'

This is a sensitive balance, especially for Gen Z and beyond born in middle and upper middle-class families. Having generally lived a comfortable life, they may not (yet) have the experience and resilience needed to rise after every fall. So, tossing them into the deep end with too much 'tough love' could backfire, leaving them feeling overwhelmed or even spiraling into serious stress or depression. But go too far the other way, and you end up with bubble-wrapped adults who might crumble at the first sign of discomfort in the outside world. Ergo the need for balance.

## Balance Between Change and Continuity

A lot of liberal thinking is about individuals freely speaking their minds to question status quo. Think Ayn Rand's celebration of the free-spirited Howard Roark who advanced creativity and challenged status quo and mediocrity.[5] While these are noble ideals that must be pursued, there is a crucial role for continuity and followership too. It ensures consistency, order and efficiency within an organization, establishing a framework for common understanding and facilitating smooth day-to-day operations and speed. Too much contrarian thinking can result in chaos, just as too much conformist behaviour can stifle innovation. Thus, a balance between the two is necessary.

On one hand, we've all heard examples of Kodak, BlackBerry, Nokia, Blockbuster or Barnes & Noble—companies that resisted change or adapted too slowly, only to have their market share devoured by more nimble players.

But too much change too fast can rattle the organization as well. Companies can lose their soul in the thirst for change. In 2011, JC Penney, a well-established American department store chain, hired Apple executive Ron Johnson as its CEO with the aim of modernizing and revitalizing the brand. Johnson implemented drastic changes, including eliminating traditional sales and discounting strategies, which alienated the company's core customer base. The company performed even more poorly under the new CEO delivering 'the worst quarter in retail history'[6] and Ron was summarily fired in 2012.

I personally witnessed this in India at a large company transitioning from promoter-led to professional management. It hired the best talent from the industry, and in the first Top 100 leadership meeting, seventy were from outside. Each came up with fresh ideas based on what they had seen work outside and started implementing them. Unfortunately, they also started looking down upon the way the company was run before and paid scant regard to the deep contextual knowledge and loyalty of the old workforce. Over the first two years of this transition, profit margins fell from 22 per cent to 14 per cent while sales growth remained mid-single digit, much lower than competitors. The multiple step-change ideas suggested by the incoming leaders were individually brilliant but were too much to be executed together. Most of those did not scale up while the investment behind them killed profitability of the enterprise. Over the next three years, the majority of these incoming leaders had either left or were asked to leave, including the CEO.

The same company, after the first few years of exploring the right balance, finally found a humble and grounded CEO who gave respect to the loyal troops, identified the core which he did not change but actually reinforced, focussed on few specific improvement projects (like new launches, cost optimization and US expansion) that really mattered and selectively chose where to learn from outside (digital for example). Over the next five years, this balanced approach helped the company regain a 23 per cent profit margin and deliver a consistent double digit growth trajectory. The share price tripled.

We need both roots for foundation and stability, and wings to explore and conquer. While this balance is commonsensical, I have personally seen leaders come in full of fresh ideas and aggressively start to drive those, but later realize that large organizations move at their own pace. Even in an outwardly poor performing business, there is a core which must not be changed and in fact should be celebrated. Change management is as much about maturity and wisdom as it is about innovation and drive.

## Balance Between Strategy and Operations

We have previously talked of two Timeless Skills: Clarity of thought, meaning being clear on strategy. And accountability, meaning bringing that strategy alive with an execution mindset. But rarely are managers able to do both dexterously.

When I worked in a Fortune 50 US MNC, the processes were set and stable. General managers were supposed to focus on strategy, governance and people development while letting the layers below manage execution. A leader spending too much time on operational details was considered not yet ready to adorn higher offices. This and similar companies produced some great leaders, but the record of these same leaders when they moved out to run other companies was mixed. An HBR article[7] studied twenty General Electric senior executives who left to become CEOs of other large companies. The authors found that without a deep knowledge of the context and deep personal relationship within the new operational network, pure strategic thinking was not enough to deliver results. Indeed, many of these stars in GE failed when they moved to a new context.

Then I joined a large Indian listed company. Processes were not so robust and there was a lot of dependence on individuals. Success entailed rolling up our sleeves and getting deep into the operations. This is a general attribute of many Indian firms. Many decades ago, US/ Europe evolved from a high growth region to low growth, and in the latter phase companies focussed on processes and profitability. So, their processes are largely set and dependence on the individual is relatively low. Indian industrial growth, however, is still relatively young, and we remain a high-growth emerging market. Many of our sectors and companies—aside from original sunrise industries like IT outsourcing and BPOs—may not have had enough time to solidify their processes. Hence leaders need to get involved in operations too. Without getting into the detail, it will be difficult to achieve success, at least in most Indian companies.

That brings the flip side risk—getting sucked up in the thick of thin things. Too much operational details, working hard every day and solving one problem after another but missing the big picture and not really moving forward with speed.

I have now come to believe in this crucial balance between strategy and operations. We have to learn to see the forest *and* the trees. Sometimes called T-shaped skills: having an overview of entire operations and the ability to zoom in where we feel things require a closer supervision. And then zoom out once things are stable and we have put a capable manager in place. So that we can again focus on the few strategic priorities without getting bogged down by day-to-day fires.

I had a vice president of Latin America who was experienced, erudite and strategic. The kind you would like to go out for wine with and have family conversations. I loved his discussions on strategy and his views on how the business could double and triple. The trouble was, he was just not delivering on his monthly targets. It was almost as if the detailed job of reviewing orders and supplies weekly and monthly was too low for him.

On the other hand, I had a vice president of the Middle East who was on top of his numbers and drove his team very hard. In his charming old-world style, he would write all sales numbers for each country to two decimal places in a black diary and could answer any questions on sales. Unfortunately, much of the Middle East was and remains a volatile region: Trade sanctions in Iran, civil war in Yemen, currency depreciation in Egypt, broken government in Lebanon . . . and so on in Iraq, Syria, Libya, etc. So, I kept asking for advance planning on how the business would move over the next three to five years, which countries we would focus on, what could go wrong in future and how would we respond. But there was limited strategic thinking, and the business became more and more difficult to run and started declining.

The first vice president left as we missed multiple quarters in a row. The second was still valuable in the current role but we were not able to give him larger responsibilities. He left us to join a smaller business.

So, if one really aspires for the highest offices, one must learn to master both strategy and operations.

## Balance Between Work and Life

Recently in India, Narayan Murthy reignited the debate on how many hours an employee should work. He urged young Indians to work seventy hours a week, recounting his own experiences as co-founder and CEO of Infosys, which is now worth USD10 billion. Multiple other companies also complained that the culture of unbridled remote working after the pandemic had started to reduce productivity and ordered employees back to office. Murthy's advice stirred up a storm, and not necessarily the good kind. Most of the internet was ready with pitchforks. Their backlash reflected the broader critique of late-stage capitalism; employees are often expected to be endlessly productive, even as the gap between corporate profits and worker compensation widens.

This debate happened at roughly the same time as the book *The 4 Hour Workweek* became a *New York Times* bestseller, selling more than two million copies. In this book, Princeton's Timothy Ferriss recounts his own experiment of checking emails only once a day, delegating most mundane tasks to a virtual assistant and selectively ignoring issues that did not really require his intervention. And achieving great success at his work despite just working four hours in an entire week (yes, not four hours a day, but four hours in the whole week).[8]

Which extreme is correct? Right or wrong, I can vouch that most senior leaders, across the globe but more specifically in Asia, work significantly more than the mandated forty hours a week. The very notion of seeking balance is often dismissed, replaced by a pervasive culture that glorifies constant hustle.

Part of it is sad since all the latest productivity measures ought to give us more free time. Are we working to live or living to work? Why, in an age of unparalleled technological advancements designed to make our lives easier, do we find ourselves more entangled in the web of work? This is the productivity paradox—the more tools we have to make us efficient, the more we seem to work. The very devices designed to liberate us from the office tether us to a perpetual cycle of emails, notifications and unending tasks, blurring the lines between professional and personal life.

The best of companies and individuals have found a careful balance between work and life, allowing structured but limited email checks, working from home, simplifying work, prioritizing and delegating. In P&G, they used to say: If anyone is consistently working more than forty to fifty hours a week, there is something wrong, either with him or his manager. When I look at my fellow corporate brethren, especially in Asia, I feel we live a very unidirectional life. Work becomes life in a classic Procrustean inversion. In Greek mythology, Procrustes had a bed where he invited travellers to rest, and then either cut or stretch their limbs to fit the bed. Beyond this seemingly macabre tale is a core lesson: We often fix the wrong variable. The bed was supposed to fit the human, not the other way around. We work supposedly to obtain the resources and challenges that can help us live a full life, to make an impact in the little time we have on Earth. Unfortunately, we often start fitting our life around work and leave little time for other pursuits. Work so long and so hard, and take so much stress, that we have little time to enjoy life. Breathtaking inanity.

What I am trying to say is best illustrated by the behaviour of people in Nordic countries, referenced before as consistently the happiest in the world. Their recipe for happiness is a rainbow of family bonding, social security, long vacations, controlled working hours and lots of outdoor activities. We have but one life, evanescent as it is, and we must enjoy all its shades.

A reminder from Naval Ravikant, the famous founder of the USD 4 billion Angellist: 'Most of the time, the person you have to become to make money is a high-anxiety, high-stress, hard-working, competitive person. When you have done that for twenty, thirty, forty, fifty years, and you suddenly make money, you can't turn it off. You've trained yourself to be a high-anxiety person. Then, you have to learn how to be happy.'

## Zorba the Buddha

We will end the discussion on balance by going back to philosophy again. In my mature years, I have started to wonder what the right balance between success and satisfaction is. The behaviour that delivers success can also lead to anxiety, and one can be successful but not really happy. Let me tell a story from a mighty intelligent man—who was as controversial as he was intriguing. His name was Osho and when asked the definition of an ideal man, he talked of Zorba the Buddha.[9]

Zorba, the famous protagonist in a Greek novel, was fun loving, lascivious, lived in the moment and represented gluttony and indulgence. Buddha, on the other hand, represents the polar opposite personality that encourages deep introspection and cautions us that desire is the root cause of all sorrow. In itself, Zorba can be entertaining but hollow—after many years of just living for the senses, most intelligent people will start questioning the larger purpose of life. In the same way, Buddha can be intellectual but dry—we may admire his wisdom, but wouldn't life be boring if we sacrifice all sensual pleasures? Osho, therefore, advocates one integrated person—unsplit and whole, encompassing the body of Zorba and the soul of Buddha. Balancing the ability to revel in the moment, savouring the flavours of life, while also cultivating the inner stillness that leads to enlightenment. To achieve balance is to acknowledge that the material and the spiritual are not adversaries but complementary forces, each enhancing the other. It is the understanding that joy and wisdom, pleasure and purpose, are *not mutually exclusive* but harmonious elements. Just as a pendulum finds equilibrium at its centre, so too does the integrated person—Zorba the Buddha—find balance in *the convergence of opposites*. An equilibrium where the laughter of Zorba resonates with the silence of Buddha.

Is this possible? In fact, Osho says that is the only way. In ancient text, Buddha was a prince who had all the luxuries—

wine, women, palaces—for most of his youth. He enjoyed them for many years but, the intelligent person that he was, started to find a life of mere senses rudderless. One night, he wakes up to find the courtesans from previous night lying in a pool of vomit. He is convulsed—what was beautiful a while ago was ugly and repulsive now. Trying to seek the true nature of reality, the meaning of life, he runs away from his comfortable home and, over time, finds enlightenment. Osho provocatively asks whether Buddha could have achieved his wisdom without first living the Zorba life? Unless you have fully lived, how can you renounce life?

Strive for a balance where desire enriches rather than dominates our human experience, allowing room for purpose and meaningful work to coexist. Osho celebrates the ideal of Krishna, always playful, always smiling, dancing with his horde of gopis (group of cowherd women who possess devotion towards Krishna). And yet, having the wisdom to propound the Bhagavad Gita, Hinduism's most prominent sacred text.

Wouldn't it be a glory if we can start living to even a small fraction of this ideal? Diligent in work, but not letting our jobs consume us. Maintaining childlike curiosity and playfulness and smile while delivering serious work at the office.

That is the balance we must aspire for.

We could go on with countless other examples of balance needed in life and in the corporate world. Balancing the physical and the digital (welcome to the era of phygital) or the balance between speed versus rigour (launching a less than robust product at speed only to then pay a heavy price with recalls). Then there's the balance between evaluation and decision-making—knowing when to stop debating and start acting; optimism and realism—staying positive in the face of challenges without veering into delusion; and conservation and economic development—preserving the planet for future generations while fostering industrial growth. It's like peeling an onion—each layer reveals another waiting to be explored.

The point is that management, and life in general, is all about finding the golden balance, an art as much as a science. Perhaps this is one more reason why computers may not be able to fully replace human leadership. The goal is often to optimize by striking a balance rather than maximize. It will be difficult for AI, driven by algorithms and data, to beat subjective human experience and evaluation.

Let us end with some lines from one of my favourite poems, *If* by Rudyard Kipling. To me, it is one of the most artistic tributes to balance:

If you can keep your head when all about you
    Are losing theirs and blaming it on you,
If you can trust yourself when all men doubt you,
    But make allowance for their doubting too;
If you can wait and not be tired by waiting,
    Or being lied about, don't deal in lies,
Or being hated, don't give way to hating,
    And yet don't look too good, nor talk too wise:
If you can dream—and not make dreams your master;
    If you can think—and not make thoughts your aim;
If you can meet with Triumph and Disaster
    And treat those two impostors just the same;
If you can talk with crowds and keep your virtue,
    Or walk with Kings—nor lose the common touch,
If neither foes nor loving friends can hurt you,
    If all men count with you, but none too much;
If you can fill the unforgiving minute
    With sixty seconds' worth of distance run,
Yours is the Earth and everything that's in it,
    And—which is more—you'll be a Man, my son!

## Summary

- Balance is very understated but crucial to success. Without it, our strengths when overdone can become our blind spots.
- Balancing confidence with empathy
  - Courage to articulate our point of view and take tough decisions while listening empathetically to others' viewpoints.
  - Striking this balance requires assertiveness, being self-assured yet not aggressive, and this skill can be learned.
- Balancing nurturing and challenging the team
  - The need for optimal stress levels for peak performance, neither too much pressure that hampers long-term performance, nor too light that people become too comfortable.
  - Balance constructive criticism with recognition of achievements to avoid pushing teams away or accepting mediocrity.
- Balancing change and continuity
  - Balance innovation with stability to avoid both chaos and stagnation. Companies fail sometimes due to resisting change but sometimes due to implementing it too rapidly.
  - Roots that give us foundation and stability, and wings to explore and conquer more.

- Balancing strategy and operations
  - Balance strategic thinking with operational involvement; mastering both to drive results effectively.
  - The forest and the trees—both matter, not just one or the other.
- Balancing work and life
  - Balance between work and personal life essential for overall well-being and productivity.
  - Procrustean inversion: Work was supposed to make life more fulfilling, but now life revolves around work.

## Food for Thought: Self-Assessment

1. Reflecting on work and life, can I identify areas where more balance is needed? Have I personally witnessed the harmful consequences of extremes, leading to the realization that the middle path is the best?

2. How can I cultivate a balance between confidence and empathy? How can I confidently articulate a point of view while also listening and understanding the other person?

3. Can I recall a time when striking a balance between challenging and nurturing others was difficult? What impact did it have on relationships and outcomes? How was the imbalance corrected?

4. Can I think of examples where too much change or too much continuity led to negative consequences, such as in the case of the Indian MNC? How can the right balance be found in my own endeavours?

5. Do I lean more towards a constant hustle culture, or do I maintain a healthy work-life balance? Am I operating within an optimal level of stress and challenge?

6.  Do I tend to focus more on the big picture or get
    bogged down in the day-to-day details? How can a
    more balanced approach to leadership be developed,
    balancing strategy and execution?

# 9

# Rejuvenation

'When you're young, you have time, you have health, but you have no money. When you're middle-aged, you have money and you have health, but you have no time. When you're old, you have money and you have time, but you have no health. So, the trifecta is trying to get all three at once'—**Naval Ravikant, founder, USD 4 billion AngelList**

'It (probably) is difficult to find happiness in oneself but it is impossible to find it anywhere else'—**Arthur Schopenhauer, German philosopher influenced by Indian thoughts**

RP was my colleague in the global management council of Cipla. She had a high stress role as president, overseeing quality in Cipla's forty-seven factories and with thousands of staff under her. This came with lots of travel, regulatory audits and friendly fires with manufacturing and commercial. When she was about to retire, some of us asked her what was next. 'I will continue working till seventy-five' was her confident reply.

Sure enough, after retiring, she joined the management council of an equally large and listed company, Dr Reddy's, again in a full-time high stress role as president—quality. And after that, she again joined an equally large and listed company Lupin in the same role. I asked her the secret of her energy and passion. 'Eat sparingly, exercise daily, dance regularly, pray and believe, don't take work stress home and sleep well.'

Work can be stressful. Relationships can be messy. Life can be difficult. High achievers will put even more pressure on themselves. Those are given. So how do we keep our sanity?

This challenge is even more pronounced in eastern cultures that traditionally score poorly on the cultural dimension of indulgence.[1] Indulgent cultures focus more on individual happiness and well-being with leisure time being a priority. Think US that scores 68/ 100 or Mexico which scores 97. The opposite is restrained cultures where societal validation supersedes individual happiness. India, along with most of Middle East and Russia, scores in twenties out of hundred.

Readers in India would remember those Sunday afternoons, gleefully playing cricket with friends in the neighbourhood. Suddenly, the jaded neighbourhood aunty peeks out from her balcony and yells, 'Bacchon, homework ho gaya?' (Kids, is the homework complete?)

Her unsolicited reminder sends a ripple of guilt through the group, and one by one, all friends start mumbling excuses to leave.

The unspoken rule is clear: Leisure comes only after every responsibility has been checked off—and maybe not even then and not even on a Sunday!

Taking time for personal renewal is perceived as a distraction from one's path. Sacrifice is given primacy, leaving little room for the idea that rejuvenation is a necessary investment for sustained success.

And yet, we know rejuvenation helps. Watch the famous Netflix documentary *Live To 100*, based on the book *Blue Zones*. The author studied five different regions of the world (specific villages in Greece, Italy, Japan, Costa Rica and USA) which had the highest concentration of people who have lived till age 100 and beyond. He found a combination of nine things that can help in longevity. These included physical movement, eating right, having the right relationships, having a purpose in life and avoiding too much stress.[2] More strikingly, along with local government, the author tried to apply some of these learnings in regular American neighbourhoods, and within months, there was a marked improvement in the entire populations' health parameters. (As an aside, in the same cultural dimension referenced above, one parameter is long-term orientation. Japan scores a perfect 100 out of 100, while USA and India score fifty and fifty-one respectively.)

In my experience, rejuvenation has five distinct pillars for sustained performance: Physical, Mental, Financial, Emotional and Spiritual.

## A: Physical

Exercise is good and not just for the body. It even has a positive impact on our brain by releasing the protein BDNF (brain-derived neurotrophic factor), helping in better learning and memory.[3] Hence, 'for the sake of your mind, exercise your body!'

My own story has been a roller coaster. I was lanky most of school and college—over 6 feet tall but weighing only 56 kilograms. My friends called me a hanger. And then I got married to a woman who was and is a brilliant chef, penning recipes on Indian delicacies in food magazines and teaching cooking on local television. And behold, within six months of marriage,

I gained twenty kilograms. I could eat a dozen gulab jamuns or motichoor ke laddoo at one go. Biryani was my gastronomic delight with a minimum serving of three plates. With chubby cheeks and the opposite of six packs, people started cautioning me to watch out.

At age thirty-five, my annual blood glucose and cholesterol reading came slightly off. Being in the pharmaceutical industry, I had read enough how, when unchecked, these seemingly minute deviations could lead to a full-blown lifestyle disease as we age. This was just the wake-up call I needed that started my fitness journey.

Fast forward by a decade. I recently did a course at a detox retreat where one's metabolic age is calculated. Mine turned out to be ten years younger than my chronological age. So, I guess my fitness regimen is working fine. It is not complicated, since I have a full-time job as a CEO and can only do what doesn't take too much time. I recount here only in the hope that some of these may make the reader's fitness journey easier. Why make the same mistakes others have made? All the below come with the caveat that exercising and nutrition, like any science, are best done under expert advice.

## Exercise

- Cardio: Recent health scares involving young executives highlight the importance of heart health. Cardio keeps our heart strong. I try to ensure 10,000 steps a day. Most of my phone calls—official and personal—are done while walking wearing earpods. On the elliptical machine, I don't even realize when thirty minutes are up, thanks to my lovely mother sharing all her daily chores. In my office, I had an exercise cycle and did one meeting a day while I was on it while my team sat at the table setting in front. My wife prefers dancing, and we go for a long walk after most dinners, so everyone can choose their own mojo. High Intensity Interval Training (HIIT) works too.

- Strength Training: Our ability to build muscle naturally weakens with age. To counteract this, resistance training with moderate weights two to three times a week is key. Cardio alone is not sufficient. Indians, with our carbs diet and low exercise, are prone to have beer belly.

- Flexibility: Just ten to fifteen minutes a day of targeted stretches or basic yoga can be a lifesaver, especially for us tall folks. Strong core muscles are great. Keeping our back loose and flexible is key to preventing that dreaded lower back pain.[4] Yoga, with its focus on mindful stretching, can significantly reduce stress and anxiety too.[5]

The most important thing to watch out for is visceral fat, the single biggest predictor of poor health.[6] BMI (Body Mass Index) is still easier to achieve (ideal is between 19–25[7]) but getting the abdominal girth to the ideal 90 per cent of hip diameter is a task.

## Nutrition

That makes us ready to dish about nutrition—the *sine qua non* in the quest for shedding those extra pounds. While exercise is crucial, the ultimate war against fat is waged in the kitchen. It's about calories in versus calories out. Unfortunately, the Indian meal might just contain too many carbohydrates (chapati, paratha, poori, rice, pulao), topped with the irresistible allure of desi sweets (because, let's face it, they are yummy).

One hearty Indian thali can pack a whopping 1800 calories—nearly an entire day's energy requirement for an adult.

Beyond weight gain, there is evidence that excess carbs and sugar can even result in cognitive decline.[8]

Cue my 'nutrition awakening'—I waved goodbye to sugar like it was yesterday's news and slashed my carbs intake by half. The initial battle with cravings was tough, but after a few weeks, the temptation dissipated. Sure, there's the occasional sweet rendezvous (tiramisu, I'm looking at you), but the irresistible cravings have long gone. Most other people have reported the same: the battle to give up carbs, as difficult as it sounds, is intense only the first few days. If we can conquer that, it becomes a way of life.

Similarly, many lunches are now Caesar salad in my office. It took a while to get used to even a single meal without roti, dal and rice. Even now, my wife insists on roti for dinner, but at least we have moved to complex carbs like ragi instead of atta (flour). At our detox retreat, they put us on a papaya and chaas (buttermilk) diet for three days, and, surprise, surprise, I loved it. The perfect antidote lunch after a heavy dinner the night before.

The one thing still missing is enough protein. We need roughly the same weight in grams of protein a day as our body weight in kilograms. For me, it meant 75 grams of protein a day. This is a basic requirement. If we are doing heavy strength or weight training, we need more to build muscle. And that is not easy. One non-vegetarian meal (say with 100 grams meat) hardly contains 20-25 grams of protein. An egg is just 6 grams protein. So, on the days of workouts, my instructor has me take a glass of protein shake that adds 22 grams protein (there are great vegan options too).

Overall, and simplistically, a meal with 25 per cent of the plate space for protein, 25 per cent for carbohydrate and remaining 50 per cent of the plate for leafy vegetables works best as a Harvard study showed.[9] There are also studies talking of mindfulness while eating: chewing slowly, enjoying every bite, deciding when to eat and even in which order (salad first, protein, fat and then carbs seems to be the current wisdom).

My biggest weakness is not knowing when to stop. We know the right strategy is to eat till we are 80 per cent full, what the Japanese call *hara hachi bu*. But since the brain only sends the 'full stomach' signal twenty minutes after eating, we keep filling our tummy even when we should stop. By the time we realize, it is too late. Hence, eating more slowly helps as does mindfulness.

And how can any discussion on food end without wine. A doctor friend told me that the French seem to have one of the lowest cardiovascular issues in the world, and this is attributed, at least partly, to their habit of having red wine in moderation.[10] In fact, when this study was aired in a popular US TV show, sales of wine in the US increased manifold. Whiskey is the Indian man's poison of choice, but after my Cape Town stint— which offers great wine and warm vineyard evenings at a very affordable price (all of USD 15 a bottle)—I have shifted to red wine, relishing a couple of glasses on weekends. Most other alcohol does more harm than good.

A balanced diet and eating in moderation are not just good for our own health but also for climate and biodiversity.

## Sleep

'Each night, when I go to sleep, I die. And the next morning, when I wake up, I am reborn'—**Mahatma Gandhi**

I am generally a poor sleeper. Any work-related stress, and the first thing I lose is sleep. There is nothing worse than lying on the bed wide awake, tossing and turning, while our partner is sleeping peacefully.

I would highly recommend the book *Why We Sleep*. The author Matthew Walker is professor of neuroscience and psychology at UCB (University of California, Berkeley), one of the world's Ivy League universities, and advocates at least seven hours of sleep a day. He says, 'Humans are not sleeping the way nature intended. The number of sleep bouts, the duration of sleep, and when sleep occurs has all been comprehensively distorted by modernity . . . The shorter your sleep, the shorter your life. The leading causes of disease and death in developed nations—diseases that are crippling health-care systems, such as heart disease, obesity, dementia, diabetes, and cancer—all have recognized causal links to a lack of sleep.'[11]

On the other hand, sleep and, specifically REM sleep, is important for memory consolidation, emotional processing, and crucial aspects of brain development.[12]

I have personally seen my concentration faltering and overall performance reducing with even minor sleep deprivation. Also, I tend to become more irritable. Few days of less sleep and the body starts showing signs of poor immune system. In my case, allergies like sneezing flare up along with a dull headache. While seven hours of sleep a day works in my case, overall sleep requirement per person may be a function of net of stress, nutrition, fitness, mental state and even spiritual quotient.

So how do we sleep better?

There is no silver bullet despite hundreds of articles written on this subject. At least in my case, I realized my sleeplessness was due to having multiple thoughts in my mind. What helped was putting a small diary near my bed to pen down these thoughts, giving a cue to the brain that it can stop worrying about them. What also helps is switching off my mobile phone at least an hour before sleep instead of the temptation to see the last email just before sleeping. Apparently, the blue light emitted by digital screens interferes with sleep-inducing hormone—melatonin. Instead of doom-scrolling on my phone, I like reading a book, taking a warm bath, or practising deep breathing. Interestingly, the thicker (read more boring) the book, the faster is the sleep. (By the way, alcohol does not help. It does make us drowsy, but one tends to wake up in the middle of the night. It also significantly suppresses high quality REM sleep)

## B: Mental

There is a part of me that loves the corporate role and the ability to create a large impact. But at the same time, a part of me wants to read and write—to understand and then distill the wisdom of great books. A part of me wants to teach—to spend time in the company of young, curious students and hopefully make a difference in their lives. A part of me wants to spend time with family—taking care of my parents and closely seeing my daughters grow. To force myself into a single role—to decide to be just one thing in life, would kill off, as Hugh Prather so beautifully said, large parts of me. Instead, why not keep being mentally sharp and occupied and be involved in more areas than one, and especially in areas beyond our corporate jobs.

Try emulating the father of management, the venerable Peter Drucker himself. Here is what he said: 'Gradually, I developed a system. I still adhere to it. Every three or four years I pick a new subject. It may be Japanese art; it may be economics. Three years of study are by no means enough to master a subject, but they are enough to understand it. So, for more than 60 years I have kept on studying one subject at a time. That not only has given me a substantial fund of knowledge. It has also forced me to be open to new disciplines and new approaches and new methods.'

My personal mojo is reading. They say 'A reader lives a thousand lives before he dies. The man who never reads lives only once.' Our dean at IIM Lucknow, who we affectionately called Rocky, introduced us to a list of 'must-read' books: not part of regular curriculum, but very helpful in our eternal quest to be 'wise.' Impressed with his advice, I have tried to read at least one book every week for twenty-five years now. Some friends started asking for a compilation and recommendation and so I created 99reads.org mentioned before. It has a list of ninety-nine books that I believe can really help us become wiser, each with a summary and review written by yours truly. There will hardly be a universal set of must-read books, since part of what makes a book memorable are our own life experiences that can relate to it. So, choose your chalice! Classics like *Animal Farm* are there and so are controversial ones like *Lolita*. There are Spanish ones (*One Hundred Years of Solitude*) and Russian ones (*War & Peace*) and African ones (*Things Fall Apart*). There are books on high science raising ultimate questions on God (*The God Delusion*), universe (*Physics of the Impossible*) and the human mind (*Incognito*)—the last few unsolved mysteries of our world. And, of course, there are books on management and self-help.

Reading seems to be a favourite habit of many successful people. Bill Gates reads fifty books every year and Warren Buffet suggested to students to read five-hundred pages a day. Elon Musk said he was 'raised by books' and spends ten hours a day reading. The North Star in reading has to be Shashi Tharoor, who, for many years, read a book a day and completed 365 before Christmas. Fiction did not count.

Beyond books, there is always the internet. I have changed my industry a few times—from FMCG to education to pharmaceuticals to medical devices. Each switch entailed many nights out to understand the new sector. Reading isn't just passive entertainment; it's a high-intensity workout for our neurons. Every intricate sentence we parse and every unfamiliar concept we grasp triggers activity in the brain. There is proven link between reading as a habit and longevity.[13]

Also, with artificial intelligence and machine learning, and general technology advancement, we know at least some of our existing skills will become obsolete. Some data suggests 87 per cent companies believe they will have serious skill gaps.[14] All the more reason to keep reading, keep learning.

## C: Financial

'Live like a poor man with lots of money'—**Pablo Picasso, famous painter and sculptor**

I did my first financial planning when I was all of eighteen. This was along with my then girlfriend, now my wife of twenty-five years. I was a lovestruck university student and asked how much money was enough before we could retire and spend time only with each other. The stretch and naive answer then was Rs 1 crore of net worth.

Those were the good old simple days. Now, most CXOs earn multiples of that every year and yet no one plans to retire soon.

For those not yet hooked onto Nassim Taleb's aphorisms, please do so. One of my favourites: 'Wealth' is meaningless and has no robust absolute measure; use instead the subtractive measure 'unwealth,' that is, the difference, at any point in time, between what you have and what you would like to have.

There are two variables. How much we have and how much we want. When I lived in Gurgaon, our neighbours were this very friendly and intelligent couple, similar in age to us. When I left for office along with the rest of the building, the couple would casually walk towards the garden with a book in hand to spend the day reading poetry. Jealous, one day, I asked the man how he could manage his expenses without working. He replied, 'You want a big car to go to places, so you have to work more years in the office. I am comfortable using the metro, so I can retire now.'

There is indeed a wisdom in frugality and a danger in living a life of excess. The famous singer Rihanna, despite all her millions in earnings, went broke. Devastated, she sued her financial adviser, citing bad financial planning advice. The advisor responded in court: 'Was it really necessary to tell her that if you spend money on things, you will end up with the things and not the money?'

Compare this with Musk who, at the height of his material success as the world's richest man, sold off his luxurious mansions and started to live in a trailer parked inside his office. 'Preparing for intergalactic life,' he had said.

Morgan Housel, the famous author of the bestselling *The Psychology of Money*, wrote to his son: 'You might think you want an expensive car, a fancy watch and a huge house. But I am telling you, you don't. What you want is respect and admiration from people and you think having expensive stuff will bring it. It almost never does—especially from the people you want to respect and admire you. Humility, kindness and empathy will bring you more respect than horsepower will.'

In fact, as we live longer and healthier, many of us fit till seventies and eighties, it raises a fundamental question. Till when will the primary pursuit of our work be about maximizing earnings? In our active life, most of us choose careers that maximize wealth creation. But at what point will we say, 'I have all these other interests in life. Now I have made enough, let me enjoy these too, since there is but one life.'

The reality of life's treadmill is what Hugh Prather, the very perceptive author of *Notes to Myself*, wisely observed: 'The number of things just outside the perimeter of my financial reach remains constant no matter how much my financial condition improves.'

## How Much Money Is Enough Money?

Let us first answer what money is good for. I still think it is great for things it can do—makes us live freely. It reduces constraints and allows freedom of choice. Many things become easier, having one less problem to worry about. It allows us much more control of our lives. Overall, a great slave, but a terrible master.

Using money to buy experiences rather than things, help others, develop or deepen relationships and save time (by hiring others to do things we don't like to do) . . . will add to our overall psychological well-being. For example, someone may like photography, and money can help buy a great camera. One may cherish being close to family, and money affords the luxury of flying everyone to one spot. One may care about making a loved one feel important and a thoughtful gift can create a magic moment.

The trouble is that we keep chasing money even when it stops giving us incremental happiness. One study[15] found 'the greater your goal for financial success, the lower your satisfaction with family life, relationship with friends and job satisfaction, regardless of household income . . . It is generally good for your happiness to have money, but toxic to your happiness to want money too much.' Maybe money boosts happiness when it is a result, not when it is the main pursuit.

So, back to how much money is enough? To each his own. One billionaire, Richard Branson, with USD 2 billion net worth preferred to buy a private Necker Island while another, Warren Buffet with USD 130 billion net worth, chooses to stay in his same modest house for the last fifty years. My simple rule is that I can retire from active employment when my savings generate enough returns to sustain my desired quality of life without needing to earn.

Wealth is having assets that earn for you while you sleep.[16] This also begs the question on how best to invest which is an entirely different book requiring expert advice. Just that basic compounding advice—aiming for reasonable (as opposed to spectacular) returns but compounded over a long period of time—is perhaps most robust. Like Buffet, avoid anything we don't fully understand, even if it is the flavour of the month.

## D: Emotional

While we now know that money alone does not give happiness, we also know what does give happiness. In a one of its kind Harvard longitudinal study spread over eighty years, the single biggest indicator of happiness was the quality of relationships.[17] 'Close relationships, more than money or fame, are what keep people happy throughout their lives.' On the other hand, 'Loneliness kills. It's as powerful as smoking or alcoholism.'

## Choosing Our Company

I lived in a hostel. In campus life, everyone found their own mate—the protective ones, the studious ones, even the idiosyncratic ones. In highs and lows, these friendships blossomed—eating together, partying together and crying together. As we spent time together, we also learnt from each other, habits began to leak, and we became more like each other. Marxists and capitalists, liberals and conservatives, atheists and God-fearing . . . all dined together, whined together . . . and subtly influenced each other.

We become the company of the people we keep. As social animals, people around us start setting the standards for what is okay and what is not. Apparently, in zoology there is a theory suggesting that you can guess the behaviour of a chimp by seeing the behaviour of the five chimps around him. Therefore, it is very important to choose our friends and significant others wisely—those who can provide challenge and comfort. We don't need too many. Just a few friends whose doors we can knock on at midnight without needing to explain. Keep asking, is this person's presence near me taking me up or taking me down. One big thing is to avoid negativity. There is so much to do in life. Time and energy are precious resources. Avoid negative people like the plague. Instead, have people around who first support us and then also gently challenge us, and help us become better than we are today.

## Hygges: Cosyness of the Soul

Finland, Denmark and Norway have consistently ranked top three happiest countries in UN surveys.[18] One of the drivers is the Danish concept of Hygges (pronounced hyoo-ga). Loosely translated, it means cosyness or granting yourself the little indulgences. Work hours typically end 3.30–4 p.m., leaving evenings free to relax: a wine with a book, a family/ friends' dinner, music or theatre. A five-week annual vacation is compulsory. Hygges is not just about having the physical time, but the mindset of granting ourselves and being grateful for the little things.

This 'me' time mindset is important not just to take a break from life's stress, but also to process it. If there is something burning inside of us, calmness comes by addressing instead of repressing emotions. Research done on type C personalities, who habitually repress their emotions, shows links to multiple illnesses including cancer.[19]

Arthur Brooks teaches one of the most loved courses at Harvard, on 'Leadership & Happiness.' He introduces a 2x2 matrix of happiness.

- One dimension is from the Greek concept eudaemonia, which is 'a good life, well lived,' living a life with a clear purpose that ties in with our values.
- The other dimension is hedonia, which means 'feeling good,' living a life with things like hygges sprinkled in so we can enjoy life too.

He advises us to strive for both eudaemonia and hedonia, both purpose and pleasure. True happiness is neither just working on purpose (it will be worthwhile, but life may become dry) nor just working on pleasure (any intelligent person will start finding it hollow). We need both—one gives meaning, the other *joie de vivre*. It is not 'either-or,' it is 'and.' Both become integrated in a full life—like having a purposeful day in office and then having a relaxing evening with special friends.

One of the popular new schools of yoga is the laughing yoga. My yoga instructor suggested we try to laugh heartily at least five times every day. Even if unnatural to start with, it usually quickly morphs into a genuine laugh. It is also very contagious. Early research suggests laughter can decrease stress hormones, release endorphins (opioid like hormones that promote feeling of well-being), reduce artery inflammation and increase HDL, the 'good' cholesterol.[20] Even the master advertiser David

Ogilvy used to say, 'The best ideas come as jokes. Make your thinking as funny as possible.' Humour is good for creativity and ironically the antidote to believers of absurdism (i.e., belief that universe is inherently irrational and chaotic). Like someone said, 'The world is a tragedy to those who feel, it is a comedy to those who think.'

## E: Spiritual

Someone asked Buddha whether he was God. He replied: 'No, I am Awake.' That is what spirituality is about—being mindful, a practical discipline for the mind and soul. To remain grounded and sane in a difficult world. Much of what happens in the world does not make moral or logical sense. Loved ones fall sick and die, bad people come to power, groups of people behave violently murdering their own species, good people often finish last. Spirituality helps us cope with this madness. Even if we are unhappy, we could still be at peace. Underneath the sadness, we can still find a deep serenity, a stillness, a sacred presence. As the Japanese author Haraki Murakami said, 'Pain is inevitable, suffering is optional.'

Isn't it ironic? All the things that give meaning and beauty to life—work, relationships, family, health, ambition—also probably give us the most stress. Dr Jon Kabat-Zinn runs the famous Stress Reduction Clinic at University of Massachusetts Medical Centre, USA. He is one of the few distinguished researchers who follow Integrative Medicine: Mind, Body, Behaviour and their wholeness and interconnectedness. His basic philosophy[21] is that stress, pain, illness, what the author calls the full catastrophe, are an inescapable reality of living.

But simple behaviour—meditating, exercising, getting enough sleep, practising altruism, nurturing relationships—is proven to significantly improve happiness and well-being. The small stuff matters. In his clinic, people showed remarkable improvement in illnesses as varied as blood sugar, cholesterol, pain, blood pressure, insomnia in the eight weeks programme, without taking any medicine. And in follow-up studies after four months, the results stayed. Even more dramatically, fMRI (functional magnetic resonance imaging) showed significant thickening (or improvement) in several regions in the brain associated with learning and memory, emotion regulation and perspective taking. On the other hand, there was a significant thinning in amygdala, the region associated with emotional and reactive responses.

So, when we say spiritual rejuvenation, we are not talking about some other fantasy world. We are talking about finding stillness and peace in this. If EQ helps us interact with other people, Spiritual Quotient or SQ helps us find and maintain our inner balance. In fact, it can become the guide to all our other intelligences because it helps us discover the real I.

## Stillness

> 'Don't speak unless you can improve on the silence'—
> **Spanish proverb**

In a world full of distractions, where we are digitally connected to everyone but ourselves, finding this stillness is not easy. I confess. I kept moving from one activity to another to 'fill' time. When it was not high intensity work, it would be adventure sports to give an adrenaline rush. Or reading or driving or binge watching or something else to keep the mind busy. The stillness of doing nothing (or trying to relish the moment) was just not my cup of tea.

As I grew older, I started craving for a little more peace, a bit more of 'no-mind' time. Call it spirituality or whatever, but this is when we can hopefully 'be one with our true self, which lies beyond our physical body, our shifting emotions and our chattering minds.'

That is when I discovered *The Power of Now*. In this momentous book, the spiritual guru Eckhart Tolle explained that the reason some people love to engage in dangerous activities is that it forces them into the Now—that intensely alive state that is free of time, free of problems, free of thinking . . . slipping away from the present moment even for a second may mean death. The issue with this approach is that the here and now experience is short-lived, hence we keep looking for the next 'jump.' But we don't need to get into adventure to reach that state, we can enter it anytime through practise and meditation.[22]

He also teaches that 'all the things that truly matter—beauty, love, creativity, joy, inner peace—arise from beyond the mind.' The challenge is that in today's materialistic world, we are always 'looking outside for scraps of pleasure or fulfilment, for validation, for security or for love.' But we tend to ignore the great treasure that lies within us and can give an experience way beyond the confines of the mundane and ordinary. Outer riches and inner poverty.

## Breathing

How important is breathing? Ancient Indian texts are replete with how much slow and mindful breathing can help.

Sri Sri Ravishankar, Indian guru and founder of Sudarshan Kriya says, 'The breath connects the body and mind. For every emotion, there is a corresponding rhythm in the breath. Just as emotions affect our patterns of breathing, we can bring about changes in our mental and behavioural patterns by altering the rhythms of our breath. It flushes out anger, anxiety, and worries, leaving the mind completely relaxed and energized.'[23]

I have been practising pranayama[24] or yogic breathing for a decade now. Anulom vilom (breathing through alternate nostrils) and Kapalbhati (aggressively breathing out) are my favourites. Personally, I feel much more relaxed and have sometimes seen my sinuses clear. I also find it easier to sleep after doing pranayama (controlled and deep breathing) just for ten minutes at night. Clinical trials are unfortunately rare for ancient Indian techniques but there are published studies linking pranayama to improved lung function, lower anxiety and better sleep.[25]

The Western world is also waking up to this lost art. 'There is nothing more essential to our health and well-being than breathing: take air in, let it out, repeat 25,000 times a day,' says the bestselling book, *Breath*. What is the way to breathe correctly? Most importantly, use your nose, not mouth. Be slow, relaxed, mindful. Practise ancient techniques like Sudarshan Kriya or Tummo. In fact, the perfect breath is this . . . 5.5 breathes per minute for a total of 5.5 litres of air.[26]

Dr Andrew Weil, the famous integrative medicine proponent who studied at Harvard Medical School, says, 'If I had to limit my advice on healthier living to just one tip, it would be simply to learn how to breathe correctly.' He popularized the 4-7-8 breathing method. Take four seconds to breathe in through your nose, hold for seven seconds, exhale in eight seconds through your mouth.[27]

## Meditation

A practical discipline to help us get into the here and now is meditation. Buddhists say that the mind is a monkey, jumping from one thought to another. Thoughts sometimes of past memories, sometimes of future events, often of our anxieties. We don't allow the present moment to just be. Meditation is perhaps our off button, to switch off this chattering. Focussing inwards to understand what is happening in our mind. When the mind is still, the seer is revealed.[28] Books have been written on it, so I won't delve much here.

The most famous method is concentrating on breathing to help us look inside. But beyond breathing, anything done mindfully can be meditation. Eating can be meditative— savouring each bite slowly, engaging all five senses—smell, taste, touch, sight, and even sound—to fully relish every morsel and observe how it nourishes the body. Walking can be meditative. So can be music, gardening, cooking, photography or reading.

I have been practising meditation for decades now. Just five to ten minutes a day. While meditating, when distracting thoughts come, as they will, be alert and *listen to the Thinker.* If you are trying not to think, who is this person, this part of you that is thinking? And who is the person, the other part of you, observing this thinker? The whole philosophy is that the real I is distinct from our intellect (thinking self), and to meditate we need to reach this real us. When distracting thoughts come, concentrate on the empty space between two thoughts and gently try going back to the breath.

## Aham Brahmasmi

Let us close by a small deliberation on the nature of this real 'us.'

In ancient Indian texts called Upanishads, also called Vedanta (literally the end or metaphorically, the highest point of Vedas), there are the four mahavakya or the four eternal truths. These include *Tat Tvam Asi*: You (God) and I are one. Or *Aham*

*Brahmasmi:* I am Brahma.[29] The spiritual idea is that the ultimate reality—whatever it is—is not different from us, we are part of each other.

My favourite Upanishad, *Kathopanishad,* says that Man minus Desire is God.[30]

*Yada sarve pramuchanyante kama ye asya hridi shrita*
*atha martyo amrit bhavati atra brahman samashnute*

When all the desires that dwell in the heart are destroyed,

Then the mortal becomes immortal and attains Brahman (the supreme reality) even here.

The famous American philosopher, Emerson, also said the same: 'Every man is a divinity in disguise, a god playing the fool!'

Yoga literally means union, of the real unadulterated us with the divine.

It is so disappointing and frustrating to see vested interests distorting this deep meaning of religion and God and replacing it with bigotry and narrow mindedness. What is sacrilegious is reducing religion to fanatic superstitions, violence and hatred in the name of an external God. There is no place in spirituality for 'my God better than your God' syndrome. The great Hillel the Elder, when asked to teach the entire Torah, explained the Golden Rule: 'What is hateful to yourself, do not do to your fellow man. That is the whole of the Torah and the remainder is just commentary.'

## Awe

Picasso used to say, 'Art washes away from the soul the dust of everyday life.' In contemplating brilliant art, say Picasso's *Guernica* or Michealangelo's *The Creation of Adam* or Dali's *The Persistence of Memory*, we get into a feeling of awe. We are inspired.

This awe can be a life altering experience. Once there was an upcoming night of a meteor shower, so my family and I slept on the roof to try and catch the sight. After being unsuccessful for hours, most of the family went down. My daughter and I stayed behind, and just as we were about to give up, we saw the most beautiful shooting star streak across the sky. It lasted just a few seconds, but we were mesmerized and spellbound. One of those shared experiences where each one knows how beautiful it was, and how futile it will be to talk about it to others. Those who have experienced it won't need explanation, they will just know. And those who haven't experienced it will hardly understand how a physical phenomenon can be so blissful.

People have recounted similar experiences about music, nature and silence. Awe helps us come out of the mundane, fathom the much bigger picture and have gratitude for all that we have been given. In the quiet moments beneath a starlit sky or amidst the brushstrokes of a masterpiece, we find solace and inspiration.

In fact, life is defined in Sanskrit as *anubhava dhara* (a stream of experiences). The experience of awe cleanses our souls and replenishes our spirits. As we navigate the corridors of corporate life, it's easy to become ensnared in the cycle of meetings and deadlines. Yet, amidst this whirlwind, may we remind ourselves about the vastness of existence and the beauty that lies beyond the confines of our daily routines.

# Summary

A: Physical rejuvenation:
- Exercise:
    - Cardio: Aim for 10,000 steps/ day
    - Strength training: Do resistance training two to three times a week
    - Flexibility: Yoga or stretching fifteen minutes a day
- Nutrition: Balanced meals of 25 per cent protein, 25 per cent carbs, 50 per cent veggies
- Over seven hours of sleep per night

B: Mental rejuvenation:
- Diversify interests, like the simple pleasure of reading, to enrich and balance life
- Adapt and evolve: Continuous learning, especially with the rise of technology like AI, crucial for staying relevant and bridging skill gaps

C: Financial rejuvenation:
- True financial freedom comes not from accumulating vast wealth but from managing desires and living within means. Simplicity over excess.
- Money is a tool for reducing constraints and increasing freedom, not a goal in itself. Strive to reach a stage where returns from assets can finance lifestyle.

D: Emotional rejuvenation:

- We become the company of people we keep. Choose friends and significant others wisely—those who can provide challenge and comfort.
- Embrace the Danish hygge—coziness of the soul, balancing life's purpose with pleasures.
- Pain is inevitable, suffering is optional.

E: Spiritual rejuvenation:

- Spirituality is about finding inner peace and connecting with ourselves and the world. It's a way to find an oasis in the chaos of our busy lives.
- Meditation and mindfulness are practices to achieve stillness. Focus on the present moment instead of the mind oscillating between the regrets of the past and the uncertainty of the future.
- Awe washes us, a wave that lifts our hearts, and awakens us to the beauty of life.

## Food for Thought: Self-Assessment

1. In what ways can I live more in the 'here and now' and reduce distraction and anxiety. (Think of ideas like replacing late-night screen time with reading a book to promote better sleep.)

2. Reflecting on the author's exploration of pursuing multiple interests beyond a corporate role, what aspects of my life bring me joy and fulfilment outside of my professional responsibilities?

3. How can Peter Drucker's approach of studying a new subject every few years be emulated to expand my knowledge and remain mentally sharp?

4. Reflecting on the anecdote of the couple choosing a simple lifestyle to retire early, how can I redefine what 'enough' truly means in my own life?

5. Given the importance of relationships for long-term happiness, how can the quality of my own connections with friends, family and loved ones be evaluated and nurtured?

6. Reflecting on the concept of spirituality as finding inner peace and stillness in a chaotic world, how can mindfulness practices like meditation or awe be incorporated into my daily routine?

# Part 3 | Conclusion and Exercises

## Afterthought

'I lead with a cool head, a warm heart and busy hands'—
**Werner Giessler, former P&G vice chairman and
one of my earliest bosses**

### Are These Skills Enough?

The first question that comes to mind is: Are these seven skills truly enough? Across multiple organizations, I have led teams tasked to identify core leadership traits that the company will value. Once deployed, each leader was assessed on those skills annually as part of appraisal and promotion cycles. I have had the privilege of exploring leadership capability models from some of the world's leading human development companies and benchmarking them against frameworks used by top MNCs and Indian firms. I have also personally done a fair bit of reading on leadership literature. Most importantly, over twenty-five years of watching promising managers succeed and fail, I have been able to correlate their success with their skill sets. Based on this experience, I feel the *Timeless Skills* framework is largely robust and complete.

That said, there is always room for variations. For example, one of the leading consulting giants presented their leadership framework to us which talked of fifty-two different leadership skills. But on closer look, most of those skills boiled down to variations of the same timeless concepts. Take, for example, 'mental rejuvenation.' One could alternatively brand it as 'learning agility,' or 'sharpening the saw'—similar core idea, different packaging. Alternately, they could be engulfed under a larger umbrella. So, we could talk of collaboration as an umbrella skill or split it into the mindset of collaboration (win-win thinking) and then the behaviour needed for collaboration (e.g. empathetic listening).

Finally, there are skills like creativity which don't make the cut in the *Timeless Skills* framework—not because they aren't valuable, but because, in my humble opinion, they aren't universally essential across all professions.

## Does Every Leader Exhibit Them?

Yes and no. The honest answer is that while most do most of the time, there are always exceptions. Steve Jobs was so creative that he could become successful despite possessing what all biographers highlight as atrocious people skills. We should not confuse between *because of* skills (that make us successful) and *in spite of* skills (despite which we are successful). The presence of Timeless Skills drastically improves the chances of success but does not guarantee it, and vice versa, since many other factors—personal and environmental—play a role too.

It is just like height and basketball. *Ceteris paribus* sure being tall would give players an edge—the US basketball team usually has an average height of 6'7", a full 8 inches higher than US male average height. But that does not completely rule out all short players, and there have been, say, 5'7" players too who compensated for their relative lack of height with speed, agility and other skills. Even within that lofty 6'7" average, one would find players ranging from a 'mere' 6 feet to a whopping 7 feet tall, who manage to deliver star results through a combination of skills.

Then, of course, there is lady luck. I meet many entrepreneurs who, alongwith their brilliance and grit, always also mention that they happened to hit upon the right idea at the right time. Many other equally gifted and tenacious people did not do as well, since at least part of the success factor is outside our control.

Pragmatically, our focus should be to control the controllables—luck or chance will happen; we just need to be more prepared.

## Living With Imperfection

I am a fan of Elon Musk. He is brilliant, he is a visionary, and he executes his ideas like crazy. He also often behaves immaturely, creates avoidable controversies on social media and treats his staff in ways a textbook manager shouldn't. He has a mercurial temper, shouting in office and firing people on the spot. His past girlfriend calls him 'a dangerous man.'

The question is: Can a man who conceives and executes audacious ideas—like the first private rocket, driverless cars, and colonizing planet Mars—who pushes forward despite widespread opposition (even Neil Armstrong, the first man on the Moon, dismissed Musk's private rocket pursuit as a complete waste), suddenly become restrained and compliant in his day-to-day life?

Wanting the brilliant side but not wanting the other aspect of the same personality—it is wishful thinking and won't happen in real life. Tesla's HR head said wisely, 'You got to take the bad with the good. Don't mess with the recipe or the magic will go away.'

And yet, often in corporate, we want everyone to be perfect, almost superhuman. We want the same person to be super passionate and innovative and a good problem-solver—and yet be willing to comply with all rules of the company, be fiercely loyal to one firm for many years and patiently wait for promotion. We will be lightning quick to point out the one area which needs improvement, while not adequately celebrating the many strengths.

I had an employee, BS. Very knowledgeable, very hard-working, coming from a family of army veterans. Took orders and gave orders and got work done in a very disciplined way. He was great in managing existing business and had the resilience to manage VUCA (volatility, uncertainty, complexity and ambiguity) countries like Yemen and Iran. But he did not ideate on new opportunities and probably did not show a strategic bent of mind. He came under me in my first year as general manager when I was also learning. In typical P&G fashion, I tried to give him feedback on his development areas and tried to 'improve' him. Instead of celebrating his many strengths, many of our conversations were centred around what was missing. In my mind, I was trying to make him better, but I pushed him so hard, I pushed him away. He resigned and joined a competing company.

There is a wealth of research on extraordinary individuals vs extraordinary teams. More and more we are realizing that instead of everyone being brilliant, we need a set of complementary individuals who can together create a winning team. This is also a more scalable model since we are less dependent on each individual. Of course, we then need to make them work together and many of the *Timeless Skills*—self-awareness, collaboration, rejuvenation—become indispensable.

We agonize too much about 'behavioural traits' of our leaders, though the truth is that the correlation is anything but a straight line, at least in the short to medium term. I've seen leaders deemed 'too soft' and others considered 'too harsh'—and both have found remarkable success in their own ways. Usually by compensating relative lack of one skill with extremely high score on another skill.

So, in the final analysis, are these skills important? Abolutely. As a practitioner of the framework, I can vouch that it has helped me in both my professional and personal life—become a better manager, a better friend and perhaps a better human being. I have consciously tried to inculcate these and whatever little success I have achieved—in career or in relationships—can be strongly attributed to my relentless pursuit of these skills.

And in that pursuit, I believe *Timeless Skills* offers a great framework.

Once again, this broad framework is hardly new, and hardly mine. It has been advocated as much by, say, Plato as by modern management gurus.

After all, some truths are simply . . . timeless.

# Notes For Self

# Notes For Self

# Notes For Self

# Learning by Teaching Exercise

At the end of every chapter, find a student (professional colleague or friend/ relative) and explain the key concepts of the chapter. Focus on what appealed to you. Then ask the student to write feedback, both on content and delivery style.

Do it for all chapters. By the time the book is completed, you should have these few pages also filled. That alone will ensure deep internalization of learnings for the reader too.

## CHAPTER 1

Student name and relation:
Student feedback:

On content (core themes as understood by the student)—

On trainer (style, passion and knowledge of trainer)—

## CHAPTER 2

Student name and relation:
Student feedback:

On content (core themes as understood by the student)—

On trainer (style, passion and knowledge of trainer)—

## CHAPTER 3

Student name and relation:
Student feedback:

On content (core themes as understood by the student)—

On trainer (style, passion and knowledge of trainer)—

## CHAPTER 4

Student name and relation:
Student feedback:

On content (core themes as understood by the student)—

On trainer (style, passion and knowledge of trainer)—

## CHAPTER 5

Student name and relation:
Student feedback:

On content (core themes as understood by the student)—

On trainer (style, passion and knowledge of trainer)—

## CHAPTER 6

Student name and relation:
Student feedback:

On content (core themes as understood by the student)—

On trainer (style, passion and knowledge of trainer)—

## CHAPTER 7

Student name and relation:
Student feedback:

On content (core themes as understood by the student)—

On trainer (style, passion and knowledge of trainer)—

# CHAPTER 8

Student name and relation:
Student feedback:

On content (core themes as understood by the student)—

On trainer (style, passion and knowledge of trainer)—

# CHAPTER 9

Student name and relation:
Student feedback:

On content (core themes as understood by the student)—

On trainer (style, passion and knowledge of trainer)—

# Examples of Learning by
# Teaching Exercise Write-Up

As you get your own learning by teaching feedback filled in the previous pages, here are some actual examples to help you prepare. The participants of the Timeless Skills workshop taught the concepts to a friend or colleague and got this written feedback from them.

1.  Participant discussed session with a colleague at work:
    'Thank you for the valuable discussion and teaching me some of the critical skills I need/lack to progress in my career. What resonated most with me was the challenge of how to manage myself. As a human resource executive for a global company, I work with many managers who are still struggling with this concept.

    Some of the biggest obstacles are:
    o   Lack of Self-Awareness
    o.  Ineffective Time Management
    o   Difficulty Setting and Prioritizing Goals
    o   Resistance to Change
    o   Poor Communication Skills
    o   Lack of Emotional Intelligence

- o   Failure to Learn from Mistakes
- o   Inability to Manage Stress
- o   Lack of Discipline and Self-Control
- o   Isolation and Lack of Networking
- o   Absence of a Growth Mindset

To overcome these challenges, individuals often benefit from developing self-management skills, seeking feedback, setting clear goals and investing in ongoing learning and personal development. Additionally, seeking support from mentors, coaches or colleagues can provide valuable insights and guidance.

These are important but fall down our list of priorities and then we stagnate in our career.

Thank you for the insights, I enjoyed the way you managed to discuss such an important topic in a very casual, comfortable manner but still made me think about how I should improve where I am lacking.'

* * *

2.   Participant had a coaching session with his fifteen-year-old daughter. Coaching a teenager involves a different approach compared to coaching an employee or an adult, but the fundamental principles of communication, encouragement and skill development still apply. Below the participant first gives background of the discussion and then appends his daughter's feedback:

We focused on her transition into taking on more responsibilities and managing her time effectively. Here's a brief overview of our discussion:

I shared with her that *Timeless Skills* are a roadmap for growing into a superhero leader in all phases of her life. That she must imagine each step on this map is a level-up in her leadership journey. Right now, it's about learning to manage herself and her responsibilities, whether it's homework, photography or hanging out with friends. As she moves forward, she will unlock new skills and face different challenges.

It's about figuring out what's important to her and creating a schedule that enables her to do all these awesome things. I emphasized that I was there to guide her through this journey, offering support and helping her navigate each challenge.

Below is her feedback:

'Hey Dad,
Our coaching session today was actually pretty cool. I liked that we talked about how I'm getting more responsibilities and stuff. It made me feel like you get what I am going through.

The part about time management was helpful. I didn't really think about setting priorities before, but I think it could make things easier. And I'm glad we're going to figure out a schedule that works for me.

It was also nice that you said we can talk about anything. Sometimes, I don't know how to bring up stuff but knowing you're there to chat makes me feel better.'

\* \* \*

3. Participant discussed learnings with a good friend who owned a business:

'It was great spending some time to discuss and align on these critical skillsets that we often assume we are doing well in but are so often overlooked.

The skills that hit home to me was my ability to delegate to my team members and trust in them that they will be accountable to execute, while I can still be confident to take responsibility and accountability for the outcome of their actions. I think I often still find myself doing things, whereas I should be delegating the responsibility to one of my team members. This directly spoke to me about my need to be better at coaching & enabling my team members.

It was also eye opening to see the difference in skill set required when managing junior people and managing senior leaders. For example, with the latter, I need to spend more time on to how we together can bridge barriers and solve problems effectively.

Overall, the way you had the discussion with me was open, relaxed and resulted in quality outcomes and some key new ways of thinking and approaching my day.'

* * *

4. Participant discussed *Timeless Skills* of listening and collaboration with his young son:

'Dear Dad, Thanks for the discussion on why it is so important to listen well, and the speaker's staff. I realize that I often interrupt others in a conversation to share my perspective without waiting for them to complete their point. I understand now that rather than listening to fully understand the others' viewpoint I'm more anxious to speak mine. From now on, I will first listen patiently until the other person has had a chance to fully complete what they want to convey and only then share my perspective with clarity. This will also allow me to understand the context of their point of view better, rather than only the content. With this, my response will also be better thought through and relevant. Another point I will keep in mind is that 'people don't care how much you know till they know how much you care.' Thanks for sharing these insights.'

* * *

5. Participant discussed some of the *Timeless Skills* concepts with her spouse. In this case, the participant wrote the summary herself:

Key points that emerged:

- My spouse said that he uses the technique of mimicking content a lot and he now understood its pitfalls
- He understood the point about high energy and time needed for good listening and hence it may not be practical to follow in every interaction
- We also discussed that sometimes probing may be done by us to get more information but if that probing is going to make the other person clamp down, it is of no use
- The basic idea is to respect the opposite person and create trust
- He shared that there was a similar concept by Napoleon Hill in *Think & Grow Rich* in which he advises to create a Mastermind group—a friendly alliance—which can help to synergize
- He pointed out that to collaborate effectively one has to give up the strong urge to control – which is high in me. So that was his advice to me, which I will bear in mind and act on

# Personal Action Planning
## Start-Stop Exercise

Based on what I read in each chapter and focussing on the themes that I personally related most with:

**Start:** What new habits or behaviour will I start in my own life?

**Stop:** What bad habits will I try to reduce or even stop?

## CHAPTER 1

**Start:**

**Stop:**

## CHAPTER 2

**Start:**

**Stop:**

# CHAPTER 3

**Start:**

**Stop:**

# CHAPTER 4

**Start:**

**Stop:**

# CHAPTER 5

**Start:**

**Stop:**

# CHAPTER 6

**Start:**

**Stop:**

# CHAPTER 7

**Start:**

**Stop:**

# CHAPTER 8

**Start:**

**Stop:**

# CHAPTER 9

**Start:**

**Stop:**

# CHAPTER 10

**Start:**

**Stop:**

# Praises from Participants
## of *Timeless Skills* Workshop

## CIPLA

'*Timeless Skills* training was offered for three hours each on the last Friday of every month. It became one of the highest rated workshops at Cipla, getting a Net Promoter Score of 94 per cent and registering a 16 per cent increase in those skills in a formal assessment of the participants before and after. Nishant's own passion in designing and then delivering the workshop was palatable. The examples shared were practical and extremely relevant. Nishant ensured participants could practice the concepts thoroughly with their teams, family, and friends'—**Nimish Dhairyawan, Cipla, Global Leadership Development, lead for the *Timeless Skills* training**

'I have tried to embrace a few key mantras from *Timeless Skills* training: a) Stress is inevitable, suffering is optional. b) Keep mornings two hours free to clarify priorities, run frameworks and scenarios and guide the team. c) Consciously avoid interrupting work to read or respond to every email that pops up. d) On Guru Purnima, I make it a point to send thank-you messages to my seniors and mentors'—**Aditi Garg, head, corporate strategy, Cipla**

'This book is a transformative guide for anyone seeking to enhance their personal and professional effectiveness. It delves deep into essential skills such as self-management, clarity of thought, accountability, collaboration and more. The training sessions were not only insightful but also highly engaging, providing practical tools. The real-life examples of individuals overcoming significant challenges by applying these timeless principles resonated with all of us. It made me realize the importance of balancing empathy and assertiveness'—**Dr Vaibhav Gaur, senior director, medical affairs, Cipla**

'The *Timeless Skills* training conducted by Nishant over six months has had a profound life-changing impact. First, the concept of clarity—knowing where we want to be—made me reflect deeply on my life and inspired me to define a personal mission. Second, realizing that we often choose to be miserable was a wake-up call. I now clearly understand what I can truly influence and have shifted from a mindset of dependence to one of interdependence. This shift has given me a profound sense of empowerment and control over my life'—**Bharat Binyani, regional head, emerging market B2B business, Cipla**

'The *Timeless Skills* course, presented by Nishant Saxena to senior managers, was an exceptional learning experience. Covering critical topics such as proactivity, self-awareness, prioritization, planning and relationship management, it provided invaluable insights. Personally, the session on *listening to understand* had a profound impact on my personal relationships, enhancing my communication skills and empathy. Professionally, the guidance on managing managers and being a functional head fostered seamless collaboration both upwards and downwards. Overall, *Timeless Skills* offered practical strategies that can be applied immediately, making it a must-attend course for anyone looking to enhance their leadership and interpersonal effectiveness'—**Jason Lee, director, Cipla Australia**

'The *Timeless Skills* journey has been truly transformative, equipping me with practical tools and valuable insights that I can apply daily in both my personal and professional life. Rooted in timeless principles from renowned researchers and authors, the course offers a strong foundation for building a purposeful and balanced life. It has inspired me to tackle challenges with greater clarity, focus and intentionality'—**Jaco Coetzee, senior director, Cipla South Africa**

## LANDMARK GROUP

The concepts of *Timeless Skills* were taught in another large company, Landmark Group (USD 7 billion retail giant based in Dubai) to a pool of over 300 finance managers. The series of workshops got an average 4.9/ 5 rating, highest ever in that company. Some verbatim feedback:

'Growing and developing people from within requires deliberate and sustained effort. *Timeless Skills* is a compelling read for everyone—from entry-level professionals to presidents, office managers to entrepreneurs, and even couples—offering invaluable insights to help individuals and teams reach new heights and avoid premature flattening of careers'—**Rajesh Garg, group chief financial and sustainability officer, Landmark Group**

'*Timeless Skills* is a holistic guide that offers practical advice for personal and professional growth. With essential skills like self-awareness, empathy and collaboration, this book provides valuable insights for navigating everyday life and achieving success'—**Rahul Bhargava, head of finance, shoe business, Landmark Group**

'*Timeless Skills* very deftly highlights how we can avoid the common "stuck in the rut" syndrome, and continue to evolve in our careers. The book highlights several blind spots that Nishant, drawing from his vast experience, has thoughtfully identified and structured for readers to benefit from. I found many valuable lessons in the book for both my professional and personal growth'—**Krishna Kumar Sarda, head of finance, lifestyle, Landmark Group**

'Nishant effectively highlighted how many people hit a plateau because they don't acquire new skills required as their careers evolve. His point about how missing skills often stem from bad habits and a lack of commitment to constant feedback and practice really resonated with me. The most valuable takeaway for me was the emphasis on self-management and accountability, and I now hold myself responsible for my own growth. Additionally, the idea that "it's not you versus me, but us versus the problem" really struck a chord. Thank you for such an inspiring and thought-provoking session'—**Surbhi Kabra, head of finance, centrepoint e-commerce, Landmark Group**

'*Timeless Skills* takes a unique approach by exploring why careers don't grow rather than just focusing on how they do. By identifying common gaps, it introduces seven timeless skills that bridge these gaps. The book structures them in a relatable and practical way, making them easily implementable. Ultimately, about growing from within, continuing to evolve and reaching one's full potential'—**Dipak Beri, head of finance, digital services, Landmark Group**

'Everyone talks about what makes careers grow, but *Timeless Skills* flips the script—it dives into why careers don't grow. Through anecdotes, it highlights the missing pieces and then lays out seven timeless skills that fill those gaps perfectly. What's surprising is that these skills are so common, yet so few people truly apply them. This book structures them in such a relatable and practical way that it just clicks'—**Raj Agarwal, manager, finance and lead for this workshop, Landmark Group**

# Acknowledgements

In Africa, they say it takes a village to raise a child. If that's true, then this book is the product of an entire intellectual township.

First and foremost, I want to thank *my father*—a true socialist at heart. He insisted on maintaining a modest household, except when it came to ideas, where reading and discussion were always encouraged. Gandhi, Nehru, Marx, Kamal Pasha—he spoke of them all, weaving the grand ideals of equality, fairness and justice into even the most mundane conversations. Partly inspired by *cogito, ergo sum* and partly eager to impress him, we did our best to become readers—and, on our more ambitious days, thinkers.

His friends were equally invested. One gifted us the entire Encyclopaedia Britannica series in the pre-Google era. Another, a Supreme Court judge, assigned us research topics (I still remember being quizzed, at age sixteen, about the Scopes 'Monkey' trial and its clash between Darwinian evolution and Biblical creation).

*My professors.* The love of reading, synthesizing, questioning, and articulating truly took root on campus. At our B-school induction, Dean Rocky handed us a list of thirty-five must-read books—not part of the MBA curriculum, but nevertheless essential in our eternal quest to be wise. Life was simpler back then, and our professors embodied this austerity.

Untouched yet by the mart of economic strife and gain, pure academic inquiry was infinitely more satisfying than flashy cars or gadgets. For my thesis, my research guides and I would escape to the terrace and spend hours drawing parallels between social revolutions and organizational transformation. Where better to discuss upheaval than under an open sky?

*My friends.* At thirty and already facing a 'mid-life crisis' (yes, they arrive early these days), my dear friend Bala and I decided the best way to find meaning was to trek to Mount Everest base camp—sans phones, with only the book, *The Story of Philosophy* for company. Avneesh Makkar was the ever-reliable sounding board for the first manuscript, and for most of life's existential dilemmas. Rajesh Garg provided a real-world testing ground with his team. Hostel life itself makes us more authentic—holding up a mirror to our flaws, insecurities and the exhausting need to be perceived as 'good'.

*My employers.* Procter & Gamble comes highly recommended for fresh graduates—early responsibility and a strong focus on the *how*. Cipla, amidst its own transformation, became a training ground to sharpen my managerial skills and witness first-hand that, in the end, execution is everything. And now, Erba—which I joined after finishing this book—provides the chance to put these learnings into action.

*My managers.* Each one left me wiser. Some offered brilliant advice, some delivered (often brutal) reality checks, and all lent a patient ear. Amit Banati, D.V. Shrimati, Paolo DeCesare, Valarie Shephard, Shantanu Khosla, Paul Miller, Kamil Hamied, Samina Hamied, Umang Vohra, Suresh Vazirani and others. If I'm still grateful to them, and connected to them, after all these years, that says a lot about their impact.

*The books I've read (and their brilliant authors).* Some books don't just inform, they shape you. *The 7 Habits* by Stephen

Covey had me so enthralled that I became its certified trainer. *The Leadership Pipeline* (Ram Charan) first taught me that careers stall because people stop learning. Will Durant showed how to distil wisdom for a wider audience, while *Animal Farm* and *Atlas Shrugged* proved that deep ideas can be wrapped in gripping prose. Richard Dawkins (*The Selfish Gene*) remains the gold standard for logical thinking and *Things Fall Apart* or *Yuganta* remind us that in any conflict, both sides are equally right (and equally wrong). These books (amongst many others) have been my silent mentors.

*My publishing team.* For over a year, Manish Kumar, the commissioning editor at Penguin, persistently nudged me to write. I kept insisting I was too busy, but he was relentless. Aninda Das, my editor, caught and corrected many errors in a draft I naively believed was final. Siya Arora, my intern from FLAME University, turned my more uninspired sentences into works of art, while preserving their original intent (case in point: 'every Om finds his Shanti').

*My family.* A CEO's role is intense as it is, and any side pursuit—like writing—demands even more time away from family. Even after twenty-five years, all my wonderful wife, Saba, asks for is more time with me, and this book unapologetically took that away. She continued to hold the whole family together with her amazing love and care for which I shall be forever grateful. My kids, however, reminded me that passion trumps practicality. Diza, despite the rigorous demands of LSE, spends hours perfecting her singing, while Saania didn't just embrace writing—she outpaced me, publishing *Teenage Chronicles* (Jaico) at sixteen. My mother (learning psychology at age seventy-five) taught us to push our limits, while my sister, Nidhi (pilot, entrepreneur, corporate leader, writer, poet—she does it all), showed that limits are mostly imaginary.

*And of course, my team.* Every career I've managed, every student I've taught, has given back as much as I've perhaps given them. Their sharp and often deceptively simple questions have forced me to think from first principles and refine my own leadership philosophy. Umang, Deepali, Nikhil, Nidhi, Devdutt, Pratik, Taher, Bharat, Aditi, Amit, Ayushi, Barkha, Anand, Akalanka, Farrah, Michael, Mark, Kabir, Richa, Ashish (I am surely missing many others) . . . from colleagues to co-travellers, we've learned together.

# The Book in a Dozen Sentences

1. Careers stagnate when we stop evolving. Growth demands learning new habits and unlearning old.
2. Leadership is an art, and the artist's greatest tool is the self. Self-management comes down to three pillars: awareness, discipline and passion.
3. Diagnose before you prescribe. Clear thinking outweighs brute effort or raw intelligence. Dig deep, beyond the symptoms. Data → Insights → Action.
4. Clear thinking is the foundation of clear communication. Master the art of the elevator pitch to convey ideas with precision and impact.
5. Focus on what matters most. Prioritize the few big things that deliver the biggest impact.
6. Take accountability. Good excuse + bad result is not equal to good result. If something is to be done, it's up to you to make it happen, and make it happen well.
7. Life isn't 100 per cent fair, but that's okay. In the long run, its fairness balances out. Focus on what you can control and play the cards dealt with.
8. It's not you versus me; it's us versus the problem. True success comes when everyone wins. Prioritize relationships over winning arguments.

9.  Listen to understand, not just to respond. Ask yourself: What might they see that I might be missing?

10. Balance is key. Strengths, when overused, can turn into weaknesses. Strive for harmony in every aspect of life.

11. Rejuvenation $\rightarrow$ Physical + Mental + Financial + Emotional + Spiritual. Nurture each one.

12. Teach to learn. Reinforce knowledge by teaching others and seeking feedback on delivery and content.

# Notes

## Preface

1. Covey, Stephen R. *The 7 Habits of Highly Effective People.* Simon & Schuster, 1989
2. Goleman, Daniel. *Emotional Intelligence.* Bantam Books, 1995
3. Charan, Ram, Stephen Drotter, and James Noel. *The Leadership Pipeline: How to Build the Leadership-Powered Company.* Jossey-Bass, 2000.
4. Goldsmith, Marshall. *What Got You Here Won't Get You There.* Hachette Books, 2006.
5. Bhagat, Rabi S., and Geert Hofstede. 'Culture's Consequences: Comparing Values, Behaviours, Institutions, and Organizations Across Nations.' Academy of Management Review 27 (3): 460. https:/ / doi.org/ 10.2307/ 4134391. 2002.
6. Peter Cappelli, Harbir Singh, Jitendra Singh and Michael Useem. Leadership Lessons from India. HBR, 2010

## Bringing It Alive

1. 'Corporations are victims of the great training robbery . . . companies spend enormous amounts of money on employee training and education - . . . close to USD 356 billion globally in 2015 alone—but they are not

getting a good return on their investment. For the most part, the learning doesn't lead to better organizational performance, because people soon revert to their old ways of doing things'.

Unknown. *Why Most Training Programmes Fail—and What to Do About It. Harvard Business Review Press*, 2016.

2. Kirkpatrick Training Evaluation Model: This talks about four levels of evaluation.

- Level 1 is immediately after the training where participants rate, on a scale of 1–5, how satisfying, relevant and engaging they found the experience. But it only tells how the participants feel about the experience. The purpose of corporate training is to improve employee performance, so while an indication that employees are enjoying the training experience may be nice, it does not tell us whether or not we are achieving our performance goal or helping the business. So Kirkpatrick went on to suggest three more levels of evaluation:
- L2: Learning or improvement in knowledge (measured through a before and after quiz).
- L3: Change in Behaviour, and
- L4: Delivery of Actual Business results.

The last two are complex to measure but the most crucial. Another good model in adrogogy (adult learning) is Kolb's 4-stage learning cycle: concrete learning (in classroom), reflective observation, conceptualization and then experimentation.

Kirkpatrick Training Evaluation Model. Donald Kirkpatrick. 1959.

3. The concept of Teaching to Learn has uncertain origins. One possible beginning was in Madras, where British

educators attempted to teach underprivileged children despite limited resources. This led them to encourage their own students to become teachers themselves. Nobel laureate Richard Feynman also contributed to this approach. He encouraged his students to explain complex topics as if they were teaching a child, using simple analogies when needed. If his students struggled to explain a concept, they were encouraged to revisit and study it further.

## Part 1: Introduction

### 1. Why Exactly Do Careers Stall?

1. Goldsmith, Marshall. *What Got You Here Won't Get You There.* Hachette Books, 2006.
2. Cain, Susan. *Quiet: The Power of Introverts in a World That Can't Stop Talking.* Crown Publishing Group, 2012.
3. Charan, Ram, Stephen Drotter, and James L. Noel. *The Leadership Pipeline: How to Build the Leadership-Powered Company.* Wiley, 2001.

### 2. So, What Can Be Done About It?

1. Learned helplessness is when, after experiencing repeated adverse situations beyond our control, we start believing we are helpless. This leads to passive behaviour and a lack of any effort to improve the situation even when opportunities for change are available. Read also about Martin Seligman's famous experiment on dogs. Those who were 'trained' to believe that they could do nothing about a shock stopped trying to escape even when they easily could and instead just lay down whining. In fact,

latest research suggests that our brain's default state may
be to assume it is helpless to change. Then this state has
to be unlearned.

2.    The Id is present from birth and is the source of all psychic
      energy. It deals with basic drives like hunger, thirst, sex and
      aggression. Freud described it as the most primitive and chaotic
      part of the personality, that pays no heed to social norms.
      Freud, Sigmund. *The Ego and the Id*, 1923.

3.    Hogan assessments are used by more than 75 per cent of
      Fortune 500 companies to evaluate talent.
      'The dark side of personality, measured by the Hogan
      Development Survey (HDS), consists of qualities that
      emerge in times of increased strain. Left unchecked, these
      can disrupt relationships, damage reputations, and derail
      people's chances of success.
      'When the pressure's on, the line between strength and
      weakness isn't always clear—drive becomes ruthless
      ambition, and attention to detail becomes micromanaging'.
      https://www.hoganassessments.com/assessment/hogan-
      development-survey

4.    Eagleman, David. *Incognito: The Secret Lives of the Brain.*
      Pantheon/Canongate, 2011.

## Part 2: Seven Timeless Skills

### 3. Self-Management

1.    Goleman, Daniel. *Emotional Intelligence.* Bantam Books, 1995.
      Daniel Goleman, the famous proponent of Emotional
      Intelligence, guided us towards EQ. And in an early
      HBR paper argued that it included Self-Awareness, Self-
      Regulation and Self-Motivation. Unfortunately, B-schools,

with an aptitude-based entrance test, oversell IQ. IQ is still important at early stages of career, but EQ becomes more and more critical for success as we grow.

2. Eurich, Tasha. *Working with People Who Aren't Self-Aware.* *Harvard Business Review*, 19 October 2018.

3. Sandberg, Sheryl. *Lean In: Women, Work, and the Will to Lead.* Alfred A. Knopf, 2013.

4. https://worldhappiness.report/ed/2024/

5. Frankl, Viktor. *Man's Search for Meaning: An Introduction to Logotherapy.* Beacon Press, 1992.

6. Covey, Stephen R. *The 7 Habits of Highly Effective People.* Simon & Schuster, 1989.

7. Carlson, Richard. *Don't Sweat the Small Stuff… and It's All Small Stuff.* Hyperion, 2006.

8. Goleman, Daniel. *What Makes a Leader.* Harvard Business Review, January 2004.

9. Murray, Henry. *Explorations in Personality.* Oxford University Press, 1938.

10. McClelland, David. 'Towards a Theory of Motive Acquisition'. *American Psychologist*, American Psychological Association, 1965.

11. Even thirty years after independence from apartheid, and despite having successive black governments, South Africa has one of the highest gini coefficients in the world, which measures the economic disparity between the rich and poor. https://en.wikipedia.org/wiki/Wealth_inequality_in_South_Africa

12. Warneken, Felix, and Michael Tomasello. *Extrinsic Rewards Undermine Altruistic Tendencies in 20-Month-Olds. Proceedings of the National Academy of Sciences of the United States of America*, 2008.

## 4. Clarity

1. Anyone who has computed Net Present Value in an excel sheet would understand this: change the terminal growth rate (generally how much will the company grow after ten years) by 2–3 per cent and the valuation changes substantially. But how would we really know eleventh year growth with that level of accuracy?

2. Dobelli, Rolf. *The Art of Thinking Clearly*. HarperCollins, 2014.

3. Index, Global Hunger. *India. Global Hunger Index (GHI) – Peer-Reviewed Annual Publication Designed to Comprehensively Measure and Track Hunger at the Global, Regional, and Country Levels.*, 13 October 2023, www.globalhungerindex.org/india.html.

4. Porter, Michael. 'What Is Strategy?' *Harvard Business Review*, Nov.–Dec. 1996.

5. Minto, Barbara. The Minto Pyramid Principle: A Powerful and Compelling Process for Producing Everyday Business Documents. McKinsey & Company, 1987

6. This anecdote has been variously ascribed to Lincoln, Woodrow Wilson, Churchill or even Mark Twain!

7. García, Héctor, and Francesc Miralles. *Ikigai: The Japanese Secret to a Long and Happy Life*. Random House, 2017.

8. Loper, Chris. *How to Use the Ikigai Diagram to Find Fulfillment. Becoming Better*, 12 January 2021.

9. Frankl, Viktor E. *Man's Search for Meaning*. Beacon Press, 2006.

10. Drucker, Peter. *Seven Personal Experiences—The Essential Drucker: The Best of Sixty Years of Peter Drucker's Essential Writings on Management*. HarperCollins Publishers, 2001.

## 5. Focus

1.   Pareto, Vilfredo. *The Pareto Principle*. Self-published, 1896. This is neatly summed up in the popular Pareto Principle, or the '80:20 Rule'. Typically 80 per cent of unfocussed effort generates only 20% of results. This means that the remaining 80% of results are achieved with only 20% of the effort. While the ratio is not always 80:20, this broad pattern of a small proportion of activity generating non-scalar returns recurs so frequently that it is the norm in many situations.

2.   Bruch, Heike. 'Beware the Busy Manager'. *Harvard Business Review*, 8 February 2023.

3.   Glaveski, Steve. '10 Quick Tips to Avoid Distractions at Work'. *Harvard Business Review*, 18 December 2019.

4.   Bregman, Peter. 'How (and Why) to Stop Multitasking'. *Harvard Business Review*, 23 July 2014.

5.   Green, William. *Richer, Wiser, Happier: How the World's Greatest Investors Win in Markets and Life*. Profile Books, 2021.

6.   Jorgenson, Eric. *The Almanack of Naval Ravikant: A Guide to Wealth and Happiness*. Magrathea Publishing, 2020.

7.   Servan-Schreiber, Jean-Louis. *The Art of Time*. Addison-Wesley, 1989.

8.   Schwartz, Tony. 'Manage Your Energy, Not Your Time'. *Harvard Business Review*, 25 September 2023.
     Quote: 'The implicit contract between organizations and their employees today is that each will try to get as much from the other as they can, as quickly as possible, and then move on without looking back. We believe that is mutually self-defeating. Both individuals and the organizations they work for end up depleted rather than enriched. Employees feel increasingly beleaguered and burned out. Organizations are forced to settle for employees who are

less than fully engaged and to constantly hire and train new people to replace those who choose to leave. We envision a new and explicit contract that benefits all parties: Organizations invest in their people across all dimensions of their lives to help them build and sustain their value. Individuals respond by bringing all their multidimensional energy wholeheartedly to work every day. Both grow in value as a result'.

9.   Covey, Stephen R. *The 7 Habits of Highly Effective People.* Simon & Schuster, 1989.

## 6. Accountability

1.   Patterson, Kerry, Joseph Grenny, Ron McMillan, Al Switzler, and David Maxfield. *Crucial Accountability: Tools for Resolving Violated Expectations, Broken Commitments, and Bad Behaviour.* McGraw-Hill Education, 2013.

2.   Saxena, Nishant, and Marius Ungerer. 'Cipla-Medpro Acquisition: The Pre- and Post-Merger Story'. *Emerald Emerging Markets Case Study*, 18 January 2019.

3.   Bossidy, Larry, and Ram Charan. *Execution – The Discipline of Getting Things Done.* Random House Business, 2002.

4.   Willink, Jocko, and Leif Babin. *Extreme Ownership: How U.S. Navy SEALs Lead and Win.* St. Martin's Press, 2015.

## 7. Collaboration

1.   *Maha Upanishad*, 600 BCE Vasudhaiva Kutumbakam.

2.   Malone, Thomas. 'Superminds: The Surprising Power of People and Computers Thinking Together'. MIT Centre of Collective Intelligence, 2018.
     Malone, who founded the MIT Centre of Collective Intelligence, explores how humans and computers can collaborate effectively. He delves into the potential of

collective intelligence, showing how it can be enhanced by integrating human and computational abilities.

3.    Gleeson, Brent. *TakingPoint: A Navy SEAL's 10 Fail Safe Principles for Leading Through Change.* Simon & Schuster, 2018.

4.    Cross, Rob, et al. 'Collaborative Overload'. *Harvard Business Review,* Jan–Feb 2016.

5.    Covey, Stephen. *The 7 Habits of Highly Effective People.* Simon & Schuster, 1989.

6.    A talking stick, also known as a speaker's staff, is a tool traditionally used in indigenous communities, particularly among the Pacific North-west nations of North America, to facilitate democratic discussions. It may be passed around during group gatherings, allowing individuals to speak one at a time
      Conflict Resolution Institute. "The Significance of the Talking Stick." *University of Denver,* December 15, 2020. https://www.du.edu/conflict-resolution/news/ significance-talking-stick

7.    Argyris, Chris, and Donald Schön. *Organizational Learning II: Theory, Method, and Practice,* Addison-Wesley Publishing Company, 1996.

8.    Cross, Rob, et al. 'Collaborative Overload'. *Harvard Business Review,* Jan–Feb 2016.

9.    Asch, Solomon E., and H. Guetzkow. "Effects of Group Pressure upon the Modification and Distortion of Judgments," Carnegie Press, 1951.

## 8. Balance

1.    *Dorland's Medical Dictionary* defines assertiveness as: 'a form of behaviour characterized by a confident declaration or affirmation of a statement…; this affirms the person's rights or point of view without either aggressively threatening the

rights of another (assuming a position of dominance) or submissively permitting another to ignore or deny one's rights or point of view'.

2. Yerkes, Robert M., and John D. Dodson. 'The Relation of Strength of Stimulus to Rapidity of Habit Formation', *Journal of Comparative Neurology and Psychology*, November 1908.

3. Overfield, Darren, and Rob Kaiser. 'One Out of Every Two Managers Is Terrible at Accountability', *Harvard Business Review*, 8 November 2012.

4. Blake, Robert, and Jane Mouton. *The Managerial Grid: The Key to Leadership Excellence*, Gulf Publishing Company, 1964.

5. Rand, Ayn. *The Fountainhead*, Bobbs-Merrill Company, 1943. Ayn Rand celebrates Howard Roark who, in her own words, 'struggles for the integrity of his creative work against every form of social opposition'. Despite initial rejection by twelve publishers for being 'too intellectual', *The Fountainhead* became a bestseller within two years.

6. Thompson, Derek. 'Who Killed JC Penney?' *The Atlantic*, 2013.

7. Groysberg, Boris, et al. 'Are Leaders Portable?' *Harvard Business Review*, May 2006.

8. Ferriss, Timothy. *The 4-Hour Workweek*, Crown Publishing Group, 2007.

9. Osho. *Zorba the Buddha*, Unknown, 1982.

## 9. Rejuvenation

1. Hofstede, Geert. 'The 6-D model of national culture', *GeertHofstede.com*, unknown, https://geerthofstede.com/culture-geert-hofstede-gert-jan-hofstede/6d-model-of-national-culture

2.    Buettner, Dan. 'The Blue Zones Secrets for Living Longer: Lessons from the Healthiest Places on Earth', *National Geographic*, 2023.

3.    'Exercise promotes the expression of brain derived neurotrophic factor (BDNF) through the action of the ketone body β-hydroxybutyrate'. Sama F Sleiman, et al. *Elife*. 2 June 2016.

      It has been known for over two decades that physical activity or neuronal activity markedly enhances BDNF gene expression in the brain (Isackson, et al. 1991; Neeper, et al. 1995) and that this increase in BDNF protein leads to activation of signalling pathways that result in exercise-dependent enhanced learning and memory formation (Vaynman, et al. 2004).

4.    George, Nils, and Stephanie Cook. 'Investigating the True Effects of Psychological Variables Measured Prior to Arthroplasty Surgery on Postsurgical Outcomes', *Journal of Pain*, 20 October 2020.

      'Impact on Flexibility and Pain, a 2020 study in the *Journal of Pain* revealed that flexibility loosens tight bands, easing chronic pain in the back, neck and shoulders.

5.    Flexibility isn't just about muscles and performance; it's a mind-body alliance. Stretching can activate your parasympathetic nervous system, promoting relaxation and calming the mind.

      'Beneficial Effects of Yoga Stretching on Salivary Stress Hormones and Parasympathetic Nerve Activity'. Nobuhiko Eda, Hironaga Ito and Takao Akama. *J Sports Sci Med*. 19(4): 695–702. December 2020.

      (In my case, like many other tall people, hamstrings— the muscles at the back of thigh—tend to tighten up, and this creates multiple problems like back and knee pain. My mantra is lying on my back on a flat hard surface, and then raising each leg to 90 degrees without bending my knee, while the other leg remains straight and horizontal. Do it five times a day and back pain disappears by day three.)

6. Visceral fat alone independently predicted risk of mortality after adjustment for the other fat measures. Waist circumference was also directly associated with mortality.

Kuk, Jennifer L., Peter T. Katzmarzyk, Milton Z. Nichaman, Timothy S. Church, Steven N. Blair, and Robert Ross. 'Visceral Fat Is an Independent Predictor of All-Cause Mortality in Men', Wiley Online Library, February 2006.

7. BMI as a simple instant measure for health: Weight in kilograms divided by the square of height in meters. Underweight: Less than 18.5. Optimum range: 18.5 to 24.9. Overweight: 25 to 29.9.

'Body Mass Index', Wikipedia, https://en.wikipedia.org/wiki/Body_mass_index

8. The link between diet and cognitive abilities is undeniable. Processed foods, high in sugar and unhealthy fats, have been shown to hamper cognitive function.

'Ultra-processed Foods – Like Cookies, Chips, Frozen Meals and Fast Food – May Contribute to Cognitive Decline'. Sara N. Burke, et al. Centre for Cognitive Aging and Memory Clinical Translational Research, University of Florida. 31 January 2023.

Two recent studies demonstrate how an ultra-processed foods heavy diet may exacerbate age-related cognitive decline and increase the risk of developing dementia.

'Association Between Consumption of Ultraprocessed Foods and Cognitive Decline'. Gonçalves, Natália Gomes, et al. JAMA Neurology. 5 December 2022.

'Association of Ultra processed Food Consumption with Risk of Dementia'. Huiping Li, et al. JAMA Neurology. 10 September 2022.

9.   'Healthy Eating Plate', Unknown, *Harvard Health Publications*, 31 January 2023.

10.  Admittedly in recent times, there have been inconsistent findings too, but generally red wine in moderation with a Mediterranean meal is recommended even by the Blue Zone study.

Renaud, S., Lorgeril, M. 'Wine, Alcohol, Platelets, and the French Paradox for Coronary Heart Disease', *The Lancet*, 20 June 1992.

11.  Walker, Matthew. *Why We Sleep*, Penguin Random House, 2017.

12.  There is a reason it is called Rapid Eye Movement. If we lift the eyelid and see the pupil of a sleeping person, it actually moves from one side to another rapidly, almost like science fiction.

Summer, Jay. 'REM Sleep Revealed: Enhance Your Sleep Quality', Sleep Foundation, 8 December 2023.

13.  Bavishi, Avni, Slade, Martin D., Levy, Becca R.. 'A Chapter a Day: Association of Book Reading with Longevity', Yale University School of Public Health, *Social Science & Medicine*, September 2016.

14.  50% of all employees will need reskilling by 2025, as adoption of technology increases, according to the World Economic Forum's Future of Jobs Report.

*The Future of Jobs Report 2023*, World Economic Forum, 21 December 2023.

15. The older article by Kahneman—suggesting happiness and wealth correlation stops after USD 75000 annual income—has now been partially debunked.

Kahneman, Daniel, Deaton, Angus. 'High Income Improves Evaluation of Life but Not Emotional Well-Being', Proceedings of the National Academy of Sciences of the United States of America, 7 September 2010.

Nickerson, Carol, Diener, Ed, Kahneman, Daniel. 'Zeroing in on the Dark Side of the American Dream: A Closer Look at the Negative Consequences of the Goal for Financial Success', *Psychological Science*, November 2003.

16. 'Seek wealth, not money or status. Wealth is having assets that earn while you sleep. Money is how we transfer time and wealth. Status is your place in the social hierarchy'.

Ravikant, Naval. *Tweetstorm: How to Get Rich (Without Getting Lucky)*, X (Formerly Twitter), 31 May 2018.

17. Mineo, Liz. 'Good Genes Are Nice, but Joy Is Better', *Harvard Gazette*, 11 April 2017.

18. The World Happiness Report, *Social Environments for World Happiness*, 20 March 2020.

19. Chapman, Benjamin P., et al. 'Emotion Suppression and Mortality Risk Over a 12-Year Follow-Up', *Journal of Psychosomatic Research* (vol. 75, no. 4), 2013.

20. Miller, Michael, MD, Fry, William F., MD. 'The Effect of Mirthful Laughter on the Human Cardiovascular System', *Med Hypotheses*, November 2009.

21. Kabat-Zinn, Jon. *Full Catastrophe Living: How to Cope with Stress, Pain and Illness Using Mindfulness Meditation*, Piatkus Books, 1990.

22. Tolle, Eckhart. *The Power of Now: A Guide to Spiritual Enlightenment*, Namaste Publishing, 1997.

23. Art of Living, *What Is Sudarshan Kriya?*, https://www.
    artofliving.org/in-en/about-us/sudarshan-kriya/what-is-
    sudarshan-kriya

24. Iyengar, B.K.S. *Light on Yoga: Yoga Dipika*. Allen and Unwin
    eBooks, 1968.
    This revered book contains an account of pranayama, and
    other yoga breathing exercises.

25. 'Anulom Vilom Pranayama: Benefits'. *Healthline*. https://
    www.healthline.com/health/anulom-vilom-pranayama#
    benefits

26. Nestor, James. *Breath: The New Science of a Lost Art*,
    Riverhead Books, 2020.

27. Cleveland Clinic, '4-7-8 Breathing', https://health.
    clevelandclinic.org/4-7-8-breathing

28. Patanjali, Maharishi. *Yoga Sutra*, ancient Indian collection
    of 195 aphorisms on yoga.

29. *Mahāvākyas*, Wikipedia, 10 March 2024.

30. Chinmayananda, Swami. 'Kathopanishad: A Dialogue with
    Death', Central Chinmaya Mission Trust, 2003.

Scan QR code to access the
Penguin Random House India website